Classification in Theory and Practice

CHANDOS
INFORMATION PROFESSIONAL SERIES

Series Editor: Ruth Rikowski
(email: rikowski@tiscali.co.uk)

Chandos' new series of books are aimed at the busy information professional. They have been specially commissioned to provide the reader with an authoritative view of current thinking. They are designed to provide easy-to-read and (most importantly) practical coverage of topics that are of interest to librarians and other information professionals. If you would like a full listing of current and forthcoming titles, please visit our web site **www.chandospublishing.com** or contact Hannah Grace-Williams on email info@chandospublishing.com or telephone number +44 (0) 1865 884447.

New authors: we are always pleased to receive ideas for new titles; if you would like to write a book for Chandos, please contact Dr Glyn Jones on email gjones@chandospublishing.com or telephone number +44 (0) 1865 884447.

Bulk orders: some organisations buy a number of copies of our books. If you are interested in doing this, we would be pleased to discuss a discount. Please contact Hannah Grace-Williams on email info@chandospublishing.com or telephone number +44 (0) 1865 884447.

Classification in Theory and Practice

SUE BATLEY

Chandos Publishing
Oxford · England · New Hampshire · USA

Chandos Publishing (Oxford) Limited
Chandos House
5 & 6 Steadys Lane
Stanton Harcourt
Oxford OX29 5RL
UK
Tel: +44 (0) 1865 884447 Fax: +44 (0) 1865 884448
Email: info@chandospublishing.com
www.chandospublishing.com

Chandos Publishing USA
3 Front Street, Suite 331
PO Box 338
Rollinsford, NH 03869
USA
Tel: 603 749 9171 Fax: 603 749 6155
Email: BizBks@aol.com

First published in Great Britain in 2005

ISBN:
1 84334 083 6 (paperback)
1 84334 094 1 (hardback)

© S. Batley, 2005

Cover images courtesy of Bytec Solutions Ltd (*www.bytecweb.com*) and David Hibberd (*DAHibberd@aol.com*).

Printed and Bound by 4Edge Limited *(www.4edge.co.uk)*

Contents

Preface

This book examines a core topic in traditional librarianship: classification. Classification has often been treated as a sub-set of cataloguing and indexing with relatively few basic textbooks concentrating solely on the theory and practice of classifying resources. This book attempts to redress the balance somewhat. The aim is to demystify a complex subject, by providing a sound theoretical underpinning, together with practical advice and promotion of practical skills.

The text is arranged into five chapters:

- *Chapter 1*: **Classification in theory and practice.** This chapter explores theories of classification in broad terms and then focuses on the basic principles of library classification, introducing readers to technical terminology and different types of classification scheme.

The next two chapters examine individual classification schemes in depth. Each scheme is explained using frequent examples to illustrate basic features. Working through the exercises provided should be enjoyable and will enable readers to gain practical skills in using the three most widely used general library classification schemes: Dewey Decimal Classification, Library of Congress Classification and Universal Decimal Classification.

- *Chapter 2*: **Classification schemes for general collections.** Dewey Decimal and Library of Congress classifications are the most useful and popular schemes for use in general libraries. The background, coverage and structure of each scheme are examined in detail in this chapter. Features of the schemes and their application are illustrated with examples.

- *Chapter 3*: **Classification schemes for specialist collections.** Dewey Decimal and Library of Congress may not provide sufficient depth of classification for specialist collections. In this chapter, classification schemes that cater to specialist needs are examined. Universal Decimal Classification is superficially very much like Dewey Decimal, but possesses features that make it a good choice for specialist libraries or special collections within general libraries. It is recognised that general schemes, no matter how deep their coverage, may not meet the classification needs of some collections. An answer may be to create a special classification scheme and this process is examined in detail here.

- *Chapter 4*: **Classifying electronic resources.** Classification has been reborn in recent years with an increasing need to organise digital information resources. A lot of work in this area has been conducted within the computer science discipline, but uses basic principles of classification and thesaurus construction. This chapter takes a broad view of theoretical and practical issues involved in creating classifications for digital resources by examining subject trees, taxonomies and ontologies.

- *Chapter 5*: **Summary.** This chapter provides a brief overview of concepts explored in depth in previous chapters.

Development of practical skills is emphasised throughout the text. It is only through using classification schemes that a deep understanding of their structure and unique features can be gained. Although all the major schemes covered in the text are available on the Web, it is recommended that hard-copy versions are used by those wishing to become acquainted with their overall structure. Recommended readings are supplied at the end of each chapter and provide useful sources of additional information and detail.

Classification demands precision and the application of analytical skills, working carefully through the examples and the practical exercises should help readers to improve these faculties. Anyone who enjoys cryptic crosswords should recognise a parallel: classification often involves taking the meaning of something apart and then reassembling it in a different way.

List of abbreviations

ASSIA	Applied Social Sciences Index and Abstracts
BC	Bliss Bibliographic Classification
CC	Colon Classification
DDC	Dewey Decimal Classification
ERIC	Educational Resources Information Center
LCBS	London Classification of Business Studies
LCC	Library of Congress Classification
OCLC	Online Computer Library Center
PMEST	Personality, Matter, Energy, Space, Time
UDC	Universal Decimal Classification

About the author

Sue Batley is a senior lecturer at London Metropolitan University and course director of the MA in Information Services Management. Her teaching and research centre upon the organisation and retrieval of information, covering traditional cataloguing and classification, and information and knowledge architecture.

Having completed a PhD on factors affecting search behaviour and retrieval of information from picture databases at the University of Aberdeen in 1989, she worked as a subject librarian and lecturer at the University of East London, before taking up her current post in 1996.

The author may be contacted as follows:

E-mail: *s.batley@londonmet.ac.uk*

Classification in theory and practice

Introduction

We have an innate ability to classify things. Classification is something we do all the time and we see examples of it all around us. So at this level classification is unconscious – we classify things to simplify our world and make sense of it.

Classification is simply about grouping together things which are alike. It is about imposing some sort of structure on our understanding of our environment. We all have our own personal classification of the world which we have developed through our experiences. One person might classify dogs under dangerous animals to be avoided; another might classify dogs as friendly animals to have around the house. Classification helps us to simplify the world.

Table 1.1 presents a classification scheme. This is how the biological sciences make sense of, or impose order on, the animal kingdom. Within the phylum *Chordata*, there is a subphylum *Vertebrata*, within that subphylum there is a class *Mammalia*, within that class there is a subclass *Theria*, within that subclass there is an infraclass *Eutheria*. This is where this hierarchy stops, but we can continue to subdivide until we reach a point where we no longer have a group, we have an individual instance. Within the infraclass *Eutheria*, we recognise an order *Primates*, within that order there is a family *Hominidae*, within that family there is a genus *Homo*, within that genus there is a species *Homo sapiens*, within that species there is you.

The phyla in the above example are like the main classes in a library classification scheme. We can recognise similarities and differences between animals within a phylum, so we can subdivide to recognise these similarities and differences. The classes within the subphylum Vertebrata all have common attributes, but we do not need taxonomic science to tell us that mammals and birds, for example, are different. We have our own

Table 1.1 Kingdom Animalia

Phylum	Subphylum	Class	Subclass	Infraclass
Protozoa				
Porifera				
Coelenterata				
Platyhelminthes				
Nematoda				
Mollusca		Cephalopoda		
		Lamellibranchia		
		Gastropoda		
Annelida				
Arthropoda		Insecta		
		Myriapoda		
		Arachnida		
		Crustacea		
Brachiopoda				
Chaetognatha				
Echinodermata				
Hemichordata				
Chordata	Urochordata			
	Cephalochordata			
	Vertebrata	Agnatha		
		Chondrichthyes		
		Osteichthyes		
		Amphibia		
		Reptilia		
		Aves		
		Mammalia	Prototheria	
			Theria	Metatheria
				Eutheria

personal classifications that tell us that sparrows and pigeons are different but that they have more in common with each other than they have with dogs. The whole point of classification is that we do not have to understand everything we experience as unique – we can place it within a structure that recognises its properties without having to make individual sense of it.

The animal kingdom classification is a very complex example of a formal classification scheme, but there are simple examples of conscious or imposed classification all around us. When we go into a record store, we notice that it has been organised according to format, with CDs, tapes, vinyl, videos and DVDs, for example, shelved separately. If we are looking for a CD we will find that they have been classified into rock and pop, dance, jazz, classical and so on. Our ability to navigate most retail outlets depends upon a shared understanding of how they are classified. Everyone has experienced frustration when a classification scheme does not meet expectations. Supermarkets can deliberately shelve items that have similarities in different parts of the store to expose customers to the widest possible range of products. This might make commercial sense in a supermarket but is not to be recommended in a library.

Library classification

We have seen that classification helps to organise, to make sense of things. It also helps us to locate things. Library classification operates on those principles, it operates to keep similar items together and separate from dissimilar items. It attempts to do this in a way that will help library users to locate the materials they need: the aim is to get the book to the reader or the reader to the book in the quickest possible time.

Library classification organises in two ways. First, it organises information itself by recognising similarities between areas of knowledge. Just like the animal kingdom classification, library classification schemes list the main and subsidiary branches of knowledge, so they provide a taxonomy of knowledge by dividing it into Social Sciences, Natural Sciences, Applied Sciences and so on. Second, library classification organises books on shelves, keeping all history books together and keeping British History near to but separate from American History, for example.

Library classification can show the distance between separate subjects by the distance between books on those subjects on the library shelves. The library becomes a physical embodiment of a knowledge structure.

It is the subject of a book that will determine its place on the library shelves. In some cases the subject of the work is obvious – the book to be classified may be a straightforward introductory text on physics, for example. Sometimes determining the subject can be rather difficult – the impact of the railways on the growth of tourism in Scotland in the nineteenth century, for example.

To keep the books in their correct order on the shelves, and bearing in mind that their order depends on their subject rather than their author or their title, the books have to be labelled in some way and the label has to identify the subject. Sometimes it would be possible to simply label the work with the subject name – say, physics – but often this would not be possible. In any event if subject names were used to establish shelf order, and assuming the logical arrangement in that case would be alphabetical, physics would be separated from related subjects like mathematics by, among others, mechanical engineering, medicine, microbiology, and music. To establish a helpful order of materials on the library shelves their subjects have to be identified by a code or system of symbols.

Library classification schemes are logical arrangements of subjects plus a system of symbols representing those subjects. All classification schemes have schedules (a list of logically arranged subjects), and all classification schemes have notations (a system of symbols representing the subjects). These are examined in detail below.

Enumerative and faceted classification

Classification schemes fall into two types – enumerative and faceted (see Table 1.2). However, major schemes do not fall neatly into one category or the other; rather, they fall somewhere on a continuum between the strictly enumerative and the strictly faceted. It is useful to examine the qualities of enumerative and faceted classification by outlining the major classification schemes in the context of their place on the continuum.

Table 1.2   Enumerative and faceted classification schemes

Enumerative	Library of Congress Classification
⇓	Dewey Decimal Classification
⇓	Universal Decimal Classification
Faceted	Bliss Bibliographic Classification
	Colon Classification

An enumerative classification scheme attempts to enumerate, or list, all subjects. There are obvious problems associated with this. Apart from the difficulty of listing everything and the resulting size of the publication, in a strictly enumerative scheme the schedule (listing of subjects) will be very long. Another problem is that subjects change and new subjects emerge that could not have been anticipated when the scheme was devised. Enumerative schemes that attempt to list all knowledge accommodate new subjects by leaving unused notations here and there to fit the new subjects into. However, it is clearly very difficult to place each new subject in its proper position among the existing subjects – the gaps in the schedule may be in the wrong place.

The most important example of an enumerative scheme is the Library of Congress Classification (LCC) which is examined in detail in Chapter 2. LCC is an exceptionally popular scheme, very widely used in the US. An attractive property of LCC is that it is relatively easy to use because the classifier simply chooses notations for topics from a comprehensive list of subjects, dispensing with the need for in-depth subject analysis.

Another example of an enumerative classification scheme is Dewey Decimal Classification (DDC), also examined in depth in Chapter 2. DDC, however, possesses features that place it closer to faceted schemes on the continuum. DDC's schedule enumerates or lists both basic and compound subjects, but the notations for many more compound subjects can be constructed using notations from other parts of the schedules or with the aid of the Tables that list common concepts like geographic area and language.

Universal Decimal Classification (UDC), examined in depth in Chapter 3, is at first glance, very similar to Dewey, from which it was developed. There are, however, important differences between the two schemes. UDC incorporates more features of faceted classification and allows for much more detailed classification than Dewey. As well as using tables of common concepts and lists of special, subject-specific, concepts to build notations, UDC allows for a notation to be built by linking the notations for independently classifiable concepts. UDC provides the classifier with much more freedom and flexibility in linking concepts than DDC. UDC was designed for use in more specialised libraries: it provides for a greater minuteness of detail because of the flexible way in which subjects can be linked together.

Faceted classification schemes do not attempt to list, or enumerate, compound subjects. Instead notations are constructed, using notations for basic subjects together with notations for common and subject-specific concepts, termed common and special isolates. This type of classification scheme is properly called analytico-synthetic, the name reflecting the two major operations involved in its use – analysis of subject and synthesis of notational elements to fully express the subject. The schedules of a faceted scheme can be quite short, because there is no attempt to list every topic. Faceted schemes are much more flexible and allow for much greater precision in expressing complex subjects than enumerative schemes and they are therefore more suitable for specialised library collections. It is relatively easy to construct a faceted classification scheme for a special collection and this is explored in Chapter 3. For the classifier faceted classification requires more thought. Enumerative schemes provide a list from which a notation can be selected, faceted schemes usually require a notation to be constructed, but the faceted approach obviously provides much more depth, freedom and flexibility. An example of a faceted classification scheme is Colon Classification (CC) which was developed by Ranganathan, whose influence on library classification is examined in Chapter 3. Another example of a faceted scheme is Henry Bliss's Bibliographic Classification (BC).

Hunter (1988) provides an overview of the advantages and disadvantages of both enumerative and faceted schemes that represents a useful starting point for further discussion and analysis.

Advantages of enumerative schemes

An enumerative scheme attempts to list all possible subjects, both simple and complex, within the defined subject field or fields. Examples are DDC and LCC.

- *Such schemes have been generally accepted and widely used with considerable success throughout the world for a long period of time.* This is arguably the main advantage of enumerative schemes. They were devised at a time when libraries were moving from closed to open access and allowing users to select their own materials direct from the shelves. As a result there was a need to organise the library stock and take-up of schemes like DDC and LCC was immediate and enthusiastic. Major libraries adopted the classification schemes and their users became familiar with the arrangement of materials and the notations. Having organised their materials using an enumerative scheme, librarians would be understandably reluctant to reclassify their stock and introduce an unfamiliar scheme.

- *A fairly short and uncomplicated notation can be used.* This is questionable. Broad subjects can usually be represented by a brief and simple notation, but more complex subjects may require expression through very long and complicated notations. DDC notations are quite elegant, using only Arabic numerals, but must be a minimum of three digits in length. LCC notations, which use both Roman letters and Arabic numerals in a mixed notation can appear complicated to users unfamiliar with them. Additionally LCC notations utilise a Cutter Number, examined in detail in Chapter 2, increasing complexity.

- *'Notationally' it is easier to display the structure of the scheme.* Notation in enumerative schemes can be very expressive. This means that the notation displays the hierarchical relationship of subjects, with brief notations for broad subjects and longer notations for more specific subjects. However, as will be seen when expressiveness is examined in the context of notation below, faceted schemes can also possess this quality. One of the major enumerative schemes, LCC, does not have an expressive notation.

Disadvantages of enumerative schemes

- *It is impossible to list every conceivable subject.* A strictly enumerative scheme would have to list every subject, no matter how detailed. For example, there would have to be a listing in the schedule for:

  Railways: Tourism: Scotland: 19th century

  Railways: Tourism: Scotland: 20th century

  Railways: Tourism: Spain: 19th century

  Every possible aspect of every subject would have to be included – clearly an impossible task. LCC has been the clearest example of an enumerative scheme for general libraries, but in recent revisions of the scheme there is increasing dependence on tables to list common concepts.

- *There can be a lack of accommodation for even simple subjects.* In practice all subjects can be accommodated, but often at the expense of helpful order or expressiveness. As will be examined below in the section on hospitality of notation, accommodating the subject of computing has been a problem for schemes like DDC. Accommodating relatively simple topics in engineering has also proved difficult (see Chapter 2).

- *New subjects cannot be accommodated and regular revision may be required.* New subjects that are inter-disciplinary in nature can often be accommodated by faceted schemes because of the flexible way in which notational elements can be combined. Enumerative schemes have a more rigid structure and may not allow notations for new topics to be built in this way. Both DDC and LCC publish regular revisions in hard-copy, which may entail reclassification of parts of the library collection. The availability of web versions of the schemes means that new subjects can be added to the schedules very quickly, so there should be little or no delay in classifying new materials correctly.

Advantages of faceted schemes

A faceted scheme lists concepts only – notations for complex subjects are built up by means of synthesis. Examples are UDC, CC and BC.

- *Because complex subjects are not listed, such schemes are easier to compile.* In Chapter 3, a faceted classification scheme for a photographic library is presented. This scheme, while by no means perfect, took only a matter of hours to compile. A faceted scheme does not have to list every possible aspect of every subject, but in listing only basic concepts can often accommodate virtually every aspect of the subject it has been designed to classify.

- *The schedules are shorter for the same reason, but, despite their brevity, they permit the classification of both very simple and very complex subjects.* The schedules of a faceted scheme can be very brief indeed. If the scheme has been created for a specialised collection, then the list of subjects may extend over only a few pages. CC, a scheme created for general libraries, is published in one small volume. The pocket edition of UDC is likewise published in a single small volume – it is truly pocket sized. Nevertheless, as will be seen in Chapter 3, when UDC is examined in detail, the depth of classification possible is very impressive.

- *New subjects can very often be catered for by the combination of already existing topics.* As was mentioned in the context of enumerative schemes, interdisciplinary subjects can often be easily accommodated in faceted schemes by the linking together of existing concepts.

Disadvantages of faceted schemes

- *The notation can become long and complex and may be unsuitable for the arrangement of documents on shelves as in a library.* It is a common assumption that enumerative schemes have simpler and briefer notations. This premise has already been questioned. There are, of course, examples of complicated notation in faceted schemes. CC's notations have become very long and complex in the 7th edition; this is to be regretted as it perpetuates the belief that faceted classification schemes are difficult to understand for library users. A carefully designed notation for a faceted scheme can be brief, simple and elegant, while achieving depth of classification.

- *The problem of citation order can cause difficulty.* Citation order is examined in detail below. Librarians as well as library users can become confused by citation and filing order in faceted schemes. Again this need not be a problem if the scheme has been designed with an emphasis on simplicity.

Notation

> Notation is the group of symbols, technically applied, which as a code represent the subjects contained in the schedules of a classification scheme in order that these subjects will be filed at the correct point in a physical sequence of subjects. (Marcella and Newton, 1994)

Notation is a feature of all classification schemes. Each concept in the classification scheme has to be assigned a notational symbol, a number, letter or other symbol, that allows that concept to be represented in 'shorthand'. In DDC, for example, the notation or the code for physics is 530; in LCC the notation for physics is QC. The function of notation is not just to indicate the precise subject content of materials; it also shows and determines the order of those materials on the library shelves. That means the notation ought to convey information about the filing order of materials on shelves and it has to convey information about the relationships between the various subjects in the collection, ensuring that related subjects are shelved together and apart from unrelated subjects.

Notational symbols can be made up of numbers and letters. One important point is that the notation has to establish a self-evident order, otherwise it would not be possible to determine what the shelf order of materials is. Numerals and letters have a self-evident order: 1,2,3; a,b,c. Numerals can be Arabic or Roman, letters can be upper or lower case. Various other symbols can be used, such as the colon, the decimal point, inverted commas, and so on. The notation may use only one of these types of symbol, or it can be a combination of some or all of the symbols listed. If a notation uses only one type of symbol then it is called a pure notation; if it uses several different types of symbols then it is called a mixed notation.

The study of notation demands an examination of a range of related concepts: simplicity, brevity, memorability, hospitality, expressiveness and flexibility. These are examined in detail below.

Simplicity and brevity

These concepts will be dealt with together because they are very closely related: a simple notation will usually be quite brief. It is obvious that simplicity and brevity are desirable in a notation. It can be argued that, from the user perspective, simplicity and brevity are the most desirable features of notation: simple and brief notations should be easy to recognise and remember. From the librarian's perspective, simple and brief notations should make shelving and shelf tidying easier.

Simplicity can be achieved by the use of appropriate symbols: the type of symbols used in the notation and how those symbols are combined. For example, in Dewey, the use of the decimal point simplifies the notation: 616.8914 is more easily recognised and remembered than 6168914. This uses exactly the same principle as when we look at and memorise phone numbers: 020 7423 0000 is much easier to remember than 02074230000. There is an excellent paper in psychology by George Miller (1956) which studies our ability to memorise things. Memorising a number, for example, of more than seven digits is difficult; we have to break the number down into chunks.

One very simple way to achieve brevity is to use letters rather than numbers in the notation. The notational base in a classification using Roman letters is 26, for Arabic numerals the base is 10. In Dewey, for example, there are 10 main classes, which makes sense working with a base of 10. If letters rather than numbers were used, up to 26 main classes could be accommodated. Marcella and Newton (1994) calculated that, using letters, 17,000 topics could be accommodated using no more than three-letter notations. If numbers are used, six-number notations would be needed to accommodate the same number of topics.

Apart from using letters rather than numbers, there are two other ways to achieve brevity: sacrifice expressiveness or sacrifice detail. Expressive notation is examined below. In an expressive notation subjects at lower levels of the taxonomic hierarchy will have longer notations. Libraries may already sacrifice detail to some extent, e.g. placing a limit on the number of digits in a Dewey class number. That may mean omitting geographical location or other details. This makes sense in terms of maintaining filing order on shelves, especially as Dewey class numbers may exceed 12 digits.

Memorability

A specific feature of notation that can assist in its memorability is use of mnemonic devices. There are two types of mnemonic device: systematic mnemonics and literal mnemonics.

Systematic mnemonics are arguably the most important aid to memory. All the major classification schemes use systematic mnemonics to some extent. Use of systematic mnemonics means that the same symbol or group of symbols is *always* used to denote the same subject concept and is *only* used to denote that subject concept. In Dewey Decimal Classification examples of systematic mnemonics can be found in the Tables. In DDC Table 1, the standard subdivision 03 represents an encyclopaedia or dictionary:

Dictionary of computing: 004.03

Dictionary of psychology: 150.3

Dictionary of climatology: 551.603

Again in DDC Table 1, the standard subdivision 09 represents a historical, geographic or persons treatment, while 41 is the notation in DDC Table 2, geographic areas, for Great Britain. Thus, if there is a book on any subject which deals with that subject from a British perspective, and there are no instructions to the contrary in the schedules, then 09 can be added to a base notation to indicate a geographic treatment, then 41 to specify Great Britain:

Non-native plants in Great Britain: 581.620941

Textile production in Great Britain: 677.0941

Zoology of Great Britain: 590.941

Unfortunately, the use of systematic mnemonics is not entirely consistent in Dewey. For example, when adding the geographic area notation for

Great Britain, usually 941 is preceded by a single zero, but sometimes two or more 0s are used and sometimes the 9 is omitted. Use of systematic mnemonics in Dewey is quite good, but can be criticised for lack of consistency. Universal Decimal Classification performs better in this respect: in UDC (41) is *always* used for Great Britain.

The second type of mnemonic device is literal mnemonics, which is the use of meaningful letters to denote a subject. This type of mnemonic device can often be found in special faceted classification schemes. An example for a science collection may be:

BIOL	Biology
CHEM	Chemistry
GEOL	Geology
MATH	Mathematics
PHYS	Physics

Notations are very easy to remember, which may be an advantage for a school library, for example.

Literal mnemonics work up to a point but often create problems. A particular problem is that the helpful order of classes tends to be lost. An example for a film library may be:

ACT	Action
ADV	Adventure
ANI	Animation
COM	Comedy
CRI	Crime
DRA	Drama
FAN	Fantasy
HIS	Historical
HOR	Horror
MUS	Musical
ROM	Romance
SCI	Science Fiction
WAR	War

In this example, Fantasy and Science Fiction films are separated, with Science Fiction located next to Romance. War and Action films are separated, with one genre at the beginning of the sequence and the other at the end. This is a very simplistic example, but it does illustrate that if literal mnemonics are used in a notation then helpful order of subjects is almost inevitably sacrificed.

Another problem is that more than one subject could be represented by the same letters. For example, in a notation for geographic areas, does AUS represent Austria or Australia? Rather than being helpful, this can be confusing for users.

Hospitality

This is essential, because without this a classification scheme would be unable to develop and respond to changes in the state of knowledge. Hospitality is the ability to accommodate new topics and concepts in their correct place in the schedules – so that their position reflects their relationship to existing subjects. Perfect hospitality would mean that every new subject could be accommodated in the most appropriate place in the schedules. In practice, schemes do manage to fit new subjects in, but not necessarily in their most appropriate place.

A rather crude way of achieving hospitality, and, as noted previously, this is used in most major enumerative classification schemes, is to simply leave gaps in the listing of subjects in the schedules – unassigned numbers or letters. The problem here, of course, is that the gaps may not be in the right places. It is very difficult to predict new subjects. The most obvious example is computing. In the 20th edition of the Dewey Decimal Classification, computing was moved to 004–006 in the Generalities class, not because that is the best place for it, but because it is the only place for it.

Hospitality in Dewey can be criticised, but it can also be praised. One way to achieve greater hospitality is to use a decimal point. If the notation only uses integers, it is difficult to expand. Gaps can be left: 120, 121, 125, 127, but the possibilities for expansion are limited. If decimal numbers are used, new numbers can be added at any point: 120, 120.1, 120.15, 120.152, 121. A notation using Roman letters can be added to in the same way of course, A, B, Ba, Baa, Bab, C. Again, using Dewey as an example, brevity tends to suffer. As new subjects are accommodated by adding numbers after the decimal point, notations get longer and longer, so relatively simple subjects like video recorders have lengthy notations: 621.38833. This has been a particular problem in the Engineering schedules because this field has developed enormously since the scheme was first devised in the 1870s.

Expressiveness

Expressiveness means that the notation reflects the structure of the schedules – it indicates the hierarchical relationship of subjects. An expressive notation will tend to convey hierarchy by having brief notations for broad subjects and longer notations for narrower subjects. An example from Colon Classification 6th edition:

D	Engineering
D8	Municipal (sanitary) engineering
D85	Water supply
D856	Distribution
D8564	Pipe
D85645	House connection

We can see how the notation indicates how the topics are hierarchically related, with municipal engineering being part of engineering, water supply being part of municipal engineering, and so on. We can also see that the narrower topics have longer notations.

Expressiveness is useful in that readers can quickly identify narrower and broader topics. Also, as it is the notation that determines the shelf order of materials, an expressive notation will facilitate browsing – materials will be shelved in a way that makes explicit the relationships between topics in a subject area. But it is important to be consistent. It is not helpful if parts of the notation are expressive and other parts are not – users will be confused if the notation seems to indicate relationships that do not exist. An unfortunate fact is that expressiveness and hospitality are mutually exclusive. The display of hierarchy will break down as new subjects are added – it might very well not be possible to insert the new subject in a place where its notation will express its relationship to other topics. For example, in Dewey, Engineering in the 620s is broken up as follows:

621	Applied physics (mechanical engineering)
622	Mining and related operations
623	Military and nautical engineering
624	Civil engineering
625	Engineering of railroads and roads
627	Hydraulic engineering

628   Sanitary and municipal engineering

629   Other branches of engineering

Electrical engineering, which was not included in the first edition of the scheme, was inserted as a subdivision of mechanical engineering at 621.3. This does not express its relationship with other forms of engineering – most of us would agree that it is at least as important as hydraulics, for example, yet its notation suggests it is of less importance.

Another argument against expressiveness is that brevity and simplicity suffer:

629	Other branches of engineering
629.1	Aerospace engineering
629.13	Aeronautics
629.134	Aircraft components and general techniques
629.1343	Parts
629.13435	Engines and fuels
629.134353	Gas-turbine and jet engines
629.1343532	Turboprop engines

This is very expressive in that it clearly shows the hierarchy of subjects, but the notations are also very long, with an 8-digit notation for aircraft engines, not a particularly complex subject in classification terms.

Flexibility

A notation is flexible if citation order can be altered to meet the needs of particular collections or users. Faceted schemes are best suited to this – the order in which the facets making up a notation are cited can be changed to meet local needs. Once a citation order has been established it has to be applied consistently. In the London Classification of Business Studies preferred citation order is alphabetical:

Advertising:	BK
Costs:	ELBC
Soft drinks industries:	KCP
Recommended citation order is:	BK/ELBC/KCP

But a library might want all the books on soft drinks industries shelved together, in which case the citation order could be changed to: KCP/BK/ELBC.

Flexibility is not only found in faceted schemes. DDC allows libraries to shelve bibliographies with their subject, by adding standard subdivision 016. Or alternatively, libraries can choose to shelve all bibliographies together at 016. For example: a bibliography of cognitive psychology:

<blockquote>016.153   or   153.016</blockquote>

Notation building

Using a strictly enumerative scheme the classifier would simply consult the comprehensive list of subjects and pick the most appropriate notation that had been assigned to the topic at hand. In faceted schemes, and also in schemes possessing some faceted features like DDC and UDC, a notation often has to be built by adding additional notational elements to a base notation.

For example, in DDC, at 727.821–0.828 Specific kinds of general libraries [727.8 = Architecture: Specific kinds of buildings: Library buildings] we find a note:

> Add to base number 727.82 the numbers following 027 in 027.1–027.8, e.g, public library buildings 727.824 ....

Turning to 027.4 we find that is the notation for public libraries. So Dewey allows the classifier to build a notation for the design of public library buildings.

UDC allows for greater freedom. Explicit instructions for the classifier are unnecessary because any two notations can be combined:

> 727 is the notation for Architecture: Buildings for educational, scientific, cultural purposes

> 027.5 is the notation for Public authority libraries

The notations can be joined by a colon to signify an equal relationship: 027.5:727 or 727:027.5

Notation building will be examined in depth in the sections on specific classification schemes in Chapters 2 and 3.

Citation order and filing order

Citation order has already been mentioned in the context of flexibility of notation. At this point it is necessary to define and explain the concepts of citation order and filing order which are examined in greater depth in the sections on UDC and faceted schemes in Chapter 3.

Citation order simply refers to the order in which notational elements are cited in a built notation. The most commonly applied rule is to cite the most specific concept first and then move in stages to the most general. Kaiser (1911) established the citation order *Concrete – Process* in an early attempt to apply consistency of citation. This obviously lacks sufficient detail for most compound topics that might have more than one concrete entity. A more detailed and useful ordering was established by Coates (1960) with his *Thing–Part–Material–Action* citation order. Obviously, not every topic would contain all these elements, but where they do all occur they should be cited in the prescribed order. For example:

Suits–Lining–Polyester–Ironing
Cars–Chassis–Aluminium–Manufacture

Ranganathan established the citation order Personality–Matter–Energy–Space–Time (PMEST) in his Colon Classification and allowed for more than one level of the personality facet or element:

Cars–Chassis–Aluminium–Manufacture–United States–1970s

Filing order, which establishes shelf order, is usually the opposite of the citation order, with general aspects of a subject shelved before more specific aspects. This makes intuitive sense: library users would expect broad aspects of a topic to be shelved before narrower aspects. Filing order obviously only becomes an issue where not all elements are present. So for the above example:

Cars	would be shelved before:
Cars–1970s	would be shelved before:
Cars–United States	would be shelved before:
Cars–Manufacture	would be shelved before:
Cars–Aluminium	would be shelved before:
Cars–Chassis	

The above formulae are difficult to apply in the arts, humanities and social sciences but similar formulae can be devised. For example:

[subject–place–time]

History–Northumberland–10th century

Filing order:

History

History–10th century

History–Northumberland

History–Northumberland–10th century

An example for a film library:

[genre–process–space–time]

Musicals–Choreography–United States–1930s

Filing order:

Musicals

Musicals–1930s

Musicals–United States

Musicals–United States–1930s

Musicals–Choreography

Musicals–Choreography–1930s

Musicals–Choreography–United States

Musicals–Choreography–United States–1930s

The issue of citation and filing order is of greatest significance in faceted schemes that allow the classifier some flexibility in the way in which concepts are combined. In enumerative schemes, citation order has been predetermined for the most part and is represented in the schedule entries. Likewise, filing order is made explicit in enumerative schemes. Using DDC, for example, notations are filed in strict number order. In schemes that use notational symbols like the colon that do not have a self-evident order like UDC and CC, then a filing order has to be specified.

Schedules

It has already been explained that the schedule of a classification scheme is simply the listing of subjects and their associated notations. It is useful at this point to examine the features of an effective schedule. As will become apparent, the schedules of the major classification schemes do not necessarily possess all these features. Rowley's (1992) criteria for an effective schedule are paraphrased and discussed below.

Coverage should be comprehensive

Whether a scheme has been designed for use in general libraries or for a highly specialised collection of materials, it is clearly essential that all relevant topics are included. As already discussed, providing comprehensive coverage is more difficult in an enumerative classification scheme, where very narrow aspects of a topic have to be explicitly catered for. In a faceted scheme it is only necessary for all relevant concepts, as opposed to compound subjects, to be listed. Providing comprehensive coverage ought to include anticipating topics that are likely to emerge. This is, of course, a very difficult task, but emerging areas of knowledge are often treated within the journal and conference literature before being written up in book form. This emphasises the importance of subject expertise and keeping up to date with new developments in knowledge.

A helpful order of subjects should be established

The schedules should bring related subjects close together to establish a helpful order of materials on shelves. Shelf order should promote browsing, with the user being able to identify and scan both broad and narrow aspects of a topic. An expressive notation helps in this respect, with the user able to browse from the general to the specific and vice versa. Helpful order is not only important within subjects but also across subjects. Subjects that have some relationship to each other should be adjacent to each other in the schedules. For example, mathematics and physics are discrete and identifiable subject areas but have a relationship in that physics is based upon, and requires an understanding of, mathematics. Mathematics and physics should therefore be adjacent to each other in the schedules to demonstrate their relationship.

New disciplines tend to be rather poorly represented in classification schemes that have a long history. Materials on subjects like women's studies and media studies are widely dispersed throughout the collection if a scheme like DDC is used. Newer disciplines tend not to restrict their sphere of interest within the traditional disciplines that were used to create main classes in DDC and other long-established schemes.

It is almost certainly the case that no classification scheme can establish a helpful order that meets the needs of all subjects and all users, but the schedules should reflect the widest possible consensus on how knowledge is structured. If a new scheme is being created to organise a specialist collection of materials, then the order of subjects within the schedule should take account of the expectations of the potential users of the collection.

There should be provision for change

This is absolutely essential. The importance of hospitality and the ability to accommodate new subjects has already been noted. As well as being able to incorporate new subjects, it is also important that changing relationships between existing subjects can be expressed. New areas of knowledge tend to be increasingly interdisciplinary and any scheme should be able to accommodate emerging topics that span existing disciplines. Faceted schemes tend to be more hospitable than enumerative schemes. As stated above, new topics can often be expressed by the combination of existing concepts in a faceted scheme, while enumerative schemes may require complete revision. Additionally, because faceted schemes can lack expressiveness, new subjects can be added without compromising the structure of the scheme as a whole. Choice of notation aids hospitality; use of decimal notation, for example allows for unlimited expansion. However, simplicity and brevity of notation will undoubtedly suffer.

As well as being able to accommodate new subjects, the schedules of classification schemes also reflect the current state of knowledge. Subjects have to be removed as well as added, and terminology used to name and describe subjects should reflect current usage. This means that regular revision is necessary.

Subject indexes

All classification schemes must have an alphabetical subject index. The schedules of the scheme are a classified subject index: subjects are presented in notation order. This means that users unfamiliar with the scheme will have to look up subject names in an alphabetically arranged listing to discover how they are represented in notation.

Two types of index can be identified: pre-coordinate and post-coordinate. The terminology may seem complex, but the distinction is simple and straightforward. A pre-coordinate index is created by an indexer coordinating terms as the index is complied. A post-coordinate index contains single-concept entries that are coordinated by the index user. When we conduct Boolean or phrase searching on a search engine like Google, we are using a post-coordinate index – we as users are coordinating the index terms as we enter our phrase or search statement.

Faceted classification schemes use the post-coordinate approach. The classifier coordinates individual concepts to create notations for compound topics. Alphabetical subject indexes to faceted classification schemes may only list simple concepts and their associated notations and so may be very brief, like the schedules themselves. Enumerative classification schemes use the pre-coordinate approach. Terms and concepts are coordinated as the scheme is compiled. Alphabetical subject indexes to enumerative classification schemes are often very detailed, displaying compound subjects and their associated notations.

Two concepts are essential in compiling an index: consistency and referencing. Consistency relates to consistent use of word form, usually the plural form of a noun is preferred, and to consistent use of citation order in combining terms. Referencing means allowing for different approaches by different users of the index, and is used to cater for synonyms and to point the user to related concepts. These issues are explored further in Chapter 4.

DDC's relative index relates subjects to disciplines. In the Dewey schedules, subjects are scattered throughout various disciplines; in the relative index, subjects are listed alphabetically with the disciplines they appear in sub-arranged under them. For example:

Chicory (Salad green)	641.3554
Agriculture	635.54
Botany	583.99
Commercial processing	664.80554
Cooking	641.6554
Food	641.3554

Some of these entries represent built notations: the numbers following 63 in the agriculture schedules have been added to specify, for example, chicory as a food from plant crops. This is a clear example of a pre-coordinate subject index.

The relative index does not include *see* references to accommodate synonyms. In all cases synonymous terms include details of the notation they relate to. For example:

Television	384.55
TV	384.55

See also references, on the other hand, are used for a variety of purposes: to cater for synonyms, to indicate broader terms and to indicate related terms. For example:

Synonym

Illumination 621.32
See also Lighting

Broader-term

Elves 398.21
See also Legendary beings

Related term

Psychiatric disorders

Medicine 616.89
See also Mental disorders

The relative index also includes qualifiers for homonyms, ambiguous terms, and initialisms and abbreviations. For example:

Homonym

Planes (Geometry)	516.154
Planes (Tools)	621.912

Ambiguous term

Engagement (Betrothal) 392.4

Initialism and abbreviation

WWW (World Wide Web) 004.678

Subject analysis

So far, we have explored subject analysis at quite an abstract level, concentrating on citation order and expression of notational elements or facets. Here a much more practical approach is used. Many new items will have already been classified by a national agency like the British Library and class numbers will be easily verified through database checking. However, this will not apply to all materials and in any event local needs may suggest an alternative location. At the very least, remotely assigned classifications should be checked. The first question any classifier should ask when adding materials to a library collection is: what is this about? The second question is: where will our users expect to find this?

Determination of subject: what is this about?

No classifier has unlimited amounts of time for subject analysis and classification of materials. In the workplace classifiers have to develop skills that will enable them to accurately and quickly determine the subject of new materials which will ensure they are shelved in their correct place among existing items. Experienced classifiers no longer have to think about the complex analytical process they are engaging in. For inexperienced classifiers there are some simple procedures to follow.

The first place to look when classifying new materials is the title of the work. In some cases this will tell the classifier everything they need to know. In a library using DDC, a work entitled *An Introduction to Psychology* will almost certainly be classified at 150. But even in apparently straightforward cases like this it is worthwhile to check the contents page. A scan of the contents may reveal that the text focuses upon educational psychology in which case it would be classed at 370.15.

In many cases the title will not include information about the subject of the work. The title of Stephen Jay Gould's *Eight Little Piggies* (1993) does not immediately suggest a work on evolution. Other title information as given in a subtitle may help to determine the subject, after which chapter and section headings as listed on the contents page should be scanned. If the nature of the work is still unclear, the brief publisher's introduction on the cover may help in determining its subject. Further assistance or confirmation can be found in the author's or editor's foreword and the introductory chapter. Other sources of information that can be consulted if necessary include publishers' blurbs and reviews.

Adapting to local needs: where will our users expect to find this?

Having determined the subject of a work, the next stage is to assign a class number to it that accurately portrays its subject content and determines its shelf location. It is often the case that a work can be legitimately classified in more than one discipline, in which case user needs have to be taken into account. For example, again using DDC, a work on the psychological testing of employees could be classified within psychology at 153.94 or within management in 658.31125. If the likely users of the work are students of psychology, then the sensible location would be with other psychology texts. If the likely users of the work are students of business administration then it should be shelved with other management texts. This is a very obvious point to make, but user needs take precedence over any other considerations. This emphasises the point that a classifier should have good subject knowledge and also a clear understanding of the needs of the collection users.

Overview

In this chapter the basic principles of classification have been introduced, emphasising its innate qualities and its familiarity. This was followed by an introduction to library classification, with an explanation of its purpose and differentiation between various types of classification scheme from the strictly enumerative to the fully faceted.

All library classification schemes have schedules, a notation and an alphabetical subject index. These, and related concepts were explored using examples from major classification schemes. Finally, practical subject analysis of materials to be classified was described with an emphasis on ensuring that shelf-arrangement meets the needs of a library's users.

An understanding of the theoretical basis of classification generally, and library classification in particular, is a necessary foundation upon which to start building practical classification skills. The purpose of this chapter was not to provide an appreciation of the deeper technical aspects of the subject, but to engender an understanding of basic principles. Anyone wishing to explore theories in greater depth can find further technical detail in the recommended readings at the end of each chapter.

References

Coates, E.J. (1960) *Subject Catalogues: Headings and Structure*. London: Library Association.

Gould, S.J. (1993) *Eight Little Piggies: Reflections in Natural History*. London: Cape.

Hunter, E.J. (1988) *Classification Made Simple*. Aldershot: Gower, pp. 58–9.

Kaiser, J. (1911) *Systematic Indexing*. London: Pitman.

Marcella, R. and Newton, R. (1994) *A New Manual of Classification*. Aldershot: Gower, p. 45.

Miller, G.A. (1956) 'The magical number seven, plus or minus two', *Psychological Review*, 63: 81–97.

Rowley, J. (1992) *Organizing Knowledge: An Introduction to Information Retrieval*, 2nd edn. Aldershot: Gower, p. 178.

Recommended reading

Bowker, G.C. and Star, S.L. (2000) *Sorting Things Out: Classification and Its Consequences*. Cambridge, MA: MIT Press.

Foskett, A.C. (1996) *The Subject Approach To Information*, 5th edn. London: Library Association.

Hunter, E.J. (2002) *Classification Made Simple*, 2nd edn. Aldershot: Ashgate.

Marcella, R. and Newton, R. (1994) *A New Manual of Classification*. Aldershot: Gower.

Rowley, J. (2000) *Organizing Knowledge: An Introduction to Managing Access to Information*, 3rd edn. Aldershot: Gower.

Hunter and Rowley provide good basic introductions to classification. Marcella and Newton provide good coverage of basic theories and the major classification schemes. Foskett is quite a difficult read, but the detail is excellent. Bowker and Star take a wider perspective, exploring basic theories and looking at classification in a range of non-library contexts.

Classification schemes for general collections

Dewey Decimal Classification

Background

Dewey Decimal Classification (DDC) is the most widely used classification scheme in the UK and indeed in the world. It was originally conceived by Melvil Dewey in 1873, with the first edition being published in 1876. The scheme is available in both print and electronic versions and is subject to continuous revision to keep pace with change. The print version, now in its 22nd edition (OCLC, 2003), is published as a four-volume set:

Volume 1   Introduction, manual, tables

Volume 2   Schedules 000–599

Volume 3   Schedules 600–999

Volume 4   Relative index

The print version struggles to keep up to date with changes in knowledge and understanding, but anyone starting to classify with DDC should use the print version in preference to the electronic version, as the overall structure of the scheme is easier to grasp. When the structure of the scheme and the principles of classifying with DDC have been mastered, then the electronic version is to be preferred because of its currency.

Coverage

DDC's coverage is comprehensive. Primary arrangement is by discipline, and within each main class a reasonable level of specificity is achieved.

Certainly depth of coverage is adequate for general library collections but libraries with more specialised collections would find DDC's general coverage and lack of flexibility a drawback. The background and cultural setting of the scheme's creator is reflected in its coverage. Much work has been concentrated upon ridding the scheme of apparent biases, but the religion schedules, for example, retain their Christian bias, with all other religions relegated to the 290s.

Dewey Decimal Classification: outline – the Hundred Divisions

000 **Computer science, information and general works**

000 Computer science, knowledge and systems

010 Bibliographies

020 Library and information sciences

030 Encyclopaedias and books of facts

040 [unassigned]

050 Magazines, journals and serials

060 Associations, organisations and museums

070 News media, journalism and publishing

080 Quotations

090 Manuscripts and rare books

100 **Philosophy and psychology**

100 Philosophy

110 Metaphysics

120 Epistemology

130 Parapsychology and occultism

140 Philosophical schools of thought

150 Psychology

160 Logic

170 Ethics

180 Ancient, medieval and eastern philosophy

190 Modern western philosophy

200 Religion

200 Religion

210 Philosophy and theory of religion

220 Bible

230 Christianity and Christian theology

240 Christian practice and observance

250 Christian pastoral practice and religious orders

260 Christian organisation, social work and worship

270 History of Christianity

280 Christian denominations

290 Other religions

300 Social sciences

300 Social sciences, sociology and anthropology

310 Statistics

320 Political science

330 Economics

340 Law

350 Public administration and military science

360 Social problems and social services

370 Education

380 Commerce, communications and transportation

390 Customs, etiquette and folklore

400 Language

400 Language

410 Linguistics

420 English and old English languages

430 German and related languages

440 French and related languages

450 Italian, Romanian and related languages

460 Spanish and Portuguese languages

470 Latin and italic languages

480   Classical and modern Greek languages

490   Other languages

500   Science

500   Science

510   Mathematics

520   Astronomy

530   Physics

540   Chemistry

550   Earth sciences and geology

560   Fossils and prehistoric life

570   Life sciences; biology

580   Plants (botany)

590   Animals (zoology)

600   Technology

600   Technology

610   Medicine and health

620   Engineering

630   Agriculture

640   Home and family management

650   Management and public relations

660   Chemical engineering

670   Manufacturing

680   Manufacture for specific uses

690   Building and construction

700   Arts and recreation

700   Arts

710   Landscaping and area planning

720   Architecture

730   Sculpture, ceramics and metalwork

740   Drawing and decorative arts

750 Painting

760 Graphic arts

770 Photography and computer art

780 Music

790 Sports, games and entertainment

800 Literature

800 Literature, rhetoric and criticism

810 American literature in English

820 English and old English literatures

830 German and related literatures

840 French and related literatures

850 Italian, Romanian and related literatures

860 Spanish and Portuguese literatures

870 Latin and Italic literatures

880 Classical and modern Greek literatures

890 Other literatures

900 History and geography

900 History

910 Geography and travel

920 Biography and genealogy

930 History of ancient world (to ca. 499)

940 History of Europe

950 History of Asia

960 History of Africa

970 History of North America

980 History of South America

990 History of other areas

Dewey Decimal Classification: tables

Table 1   Standard subdivisions

Table 2   Geographic areas, historical periods, persons

Table 3   Subdivisions for the arts, for individual literatures, for specific literary forms

Table 3*A*   Subdivisions for works by or about individual authors

Table 3*B*   Subdivisions for works by or about more than one author

Table 3*C*   Notation to be added where instructed in Table 3*B*, 700.4, 791.4, 808–9

Table 4   Subdivisions of individual languages and language families

Table 5   Ethnic and national groups

Table 6   Languages

Changes from DDC21

Much of the terminology has changed in the 22nd edition. It has been brought up to date, with some of the more archaic terms not in general use replaced by more readily understandable and recognisable terminology. That is to be welcomed. For example, Palaeontology and palaeozoology has been replaced by Fossils and prehistoric life. The main class 'Generalities' has also been renamed: Computer science, information and general works. This solves the semantic problem of computing being a generality – its position in the scheme still does not reflect its relationship with other topics and its promotion to main class status can be questioned, but it is a sensible compromise.

Table 7: Groups of Persons has disappeared. Much of the table, i.e. persons by occupational characteristics, simply reproduced notations for subjects listed in the main schedules, and persons by various non-occupational characteristics reproduced the 'history and description with respect to kinds of persons' in Table 1, so this seems to be a sensible move.

Structure and use

DDC is arranged into 10 main classes, 100 divisions and 1,000 sections.

DDC: The 10 main classes

000   Computer science, information and general works

100   Philosophy and psychology

200 Religion

300 Social sciences

400 Language

500 Science

600 Technology

700 Arts and recreation

800 Literature

900 History and geography

Each main class is divided into 10 divisions:

100 Philosophy

110 Metaphysics

120 Epistemology

130 Parapsychology and occultism

140 Philosophical schools of thought

150 Psychology

160 Logic

170 Ethics

180 Ancient, medieval and eastern philosophy

190 Modern western philosophy

Each division is subdivided into 10 sections:

140 Specific philosophical schools

141 Idealism and related systems

142 Critical philosophy

143 Bergsonism and intuitionism

144 Humanism and related systems

145 Sensationalism

146 Naturalism and related systems

147 Pantheism and related systems

148 Eclecticism, liberalism and traditionalism

149 Other philosophical systems

Each of the 1,000 sections that has subdivisions extending over more than two pages has a summary. For example:

155   Differential and developmental psychology

Summary

155.2   Individual psychology

155.3   Sex psychology and psychology of the sexes

155.4   Child psychology

155.5   Psychology of young people twelve to twenty

155.6   Psychology of adults

155.7   Evolutional psychology

155.8   Ethnopsychology and national psychology

155.9   Environmental psychology

In the schedules, the 1,000 sections are listed separately, followed in detail by any subdivisions they might have. This works quite well generally, but of course not every subject can be subdivided and re-subdivided into groups of 10.

The schedules only rarely list notations with more than four numbers after the decimal point, although in rapidly expanding disciplines like engineering you can find some very lengthy notations for relatively simple concepts, for example: commercial airplanes: 629.133340423. However, in general, instructions tell the classifier how to build longer numbers for more specific subjects. Example:

025.46 classification of specific disciplines and subjects

> Add to base number 025.46 notation 001-999, e.g. classification of education 025.4637

This is a major strength of DDC. It does not attempt to list absolutely everything, which means that the schedules are long, but nothing like as long as they would be if everything was listed.

Notes

The notes in the schedules are essential sources of information for the classifier. There are four types of notes in DDC22.

- notes that describe what is found in a class;
- including notes (notes that identify topics in 'standing-room');

- notes that describe what is found in other classes;
- notes that explain changes or irregularities in schedules and tables.

Obviously each of these need to be fully explained.

Notes that describe what is found in a class

Definition notes

These notes help to clarify the meaning of terms in the schedules. Examples:

529.7   Horology

Finding and measuring time

781.62   Folk music

Music indigenous to the cultural group in which it occurs, usually evolved through aural transmission

Scope notes

These notes indicate the breadth of meaning of a heading in the schedules. Examples:

155.4   Child psychology

Through age eleven

651.3741   Secretarial services

Work of secretaries, stenographers, typists

'Former heading' notes

These notes are rare and self-explanatory. They are only given when a heading has changed significantly (i.e. it is not immediately recognisable as representing the same concept) from one edition to the next. Examples:

212.6   Ways of knowing God

Former heading: Knowability

615.88   Traditional remedies

Former heading: Empirical and historical remedies

'Former name' notes

These notes are self-explanatory and rather rare in the schedules (you will find most examples in the Geographic Areas Table). They simply indicate a change in terminology. The class number is unchanged, the concept is unchanged. Examples:

> 341.552   International Court of Justice
>
>> Former name: Permanent Court of International Justice
>
> 583.64   Capparales
>
>> Former name: Capparidales

'Variant name' notes

Again, these notes are self-explanatory. They are used to identify synonyms or near synonyms. Examples:

> 588.2   Bryopsida
>
>> Variant names: Musci, mosses
>
> 621.38456 Cellular telephone systems
>
>> Variant names: cellular radio, portable telephone systems

'Class-here' notes

Like scope notes, these tell you what topics are included in a class. Examples:

> 025.524   Information search and retrieval
>
>> Class here search strategy
>
> 658.4038 Information management
>
>> Class here gathering of information by management for use in managerial decision making; information resources, knowledge management

They can also serve to indicate where interdisciplinary or comprehensive works are to be classified. Examples:

> 027.662   Hospital libraries
>
>> Class here comprehensive works on patients' and medical libraries

615.822   Therapeutic massage

           Class here interdisciplinary works on massage

Including notes (notes that identify topics in 'standing-room')

These notes provide a location for topics that do not generate enough literature (at least not yet) to justify assigning them a separate number. The assumption is that at some future date the topics could be assigned their own number. Because of this, topics in standing room do not have the capacity to be added to – you cannot add standard subdivisions or apply any other form of number building. There is a good, pragmatic reason for this – if the number for the topic in standing room has not been added to, then a new number for a topic can be created simply by adding one digit. It is probably best to illustrate with examples.

154.4   Altered states of consciousness

           Including altered states due to use of drugs; hallucinations

025.313   Form (of catalogue)

           Including card catalogues

025.3132   Online catalogues

Online catalogues have been taken out of standing room and assigned their own number.

Rather confusingly, there are two other types of 'including' note that are only to be found in the taxonomic schedules (579–590). These do not denote topics in standing room, and in fact there are explicit instructions about how to number build. The first type of 'including' note in the taxonomic schedules lists scientific nomenclature, the second lists common and genus names. At some classes both types of 'including' note are present, at some classes only one type is given. Examples:

579.565   Plectomycetes

           Including Gymnascales, Microascales, Onygenales

598.864   Corvidae

           Including crows, jays, magpies, ravens, rooks

584.38   Iridales

Including Burmanniaceae

Including blackberry, lily, crocuses, freesias, gladiolus (sword lilies), saffron, tigerflowers

Notes that describe what is found in other classes

'Class elsewhere' notes

These notes always begin with the word 'class' and lead the classifier to a preferred number for related topics and/or to a comprehensive number for interdisciplinary works. This is an extremely useful device as the classifier may have overlooked an alternative (preferred) location for a work. Examples:

657.3   Financial reports (financial statements)

Class use of financial reports by management to improve business performance in 658.1512

337.1   Multilateral economic cooperation

Class bilateral economic cooperation in 337.3–337.9; class interdisciplinary works on intergovernmental organisations in 341.2

'See' notes

In the main schedules these notes always begin with 'for' and are always in italics. They lead the classifier to an alternative location for narrower aspects of a topic, and may also indicate how a concept is represented in other disciplines. Examples:

358.3   Chemical, biological, radiological warfare

For Nuclear warfare, see 355.0217. For a specific aspect of weapons of mass destruction, see the aspect, e.g. Disarmament of weapons of mass destruction 327.1745

792.78   Theatrical dancing

For dancing in musical plays, see 792.62

'See also' notes

Again, these notes are always italicised and always begin 'see also'. They lead the classifier to related topics, often in other disciplines. Examples:

306.82   Patterns in mate selection

See also 392.4 for the Customs of mate selection; also 646.77 for Practical guidance on choosing a mate and dating behaviour

618.242   Dietetics and nutrition for pregnant women

See also 641.56319 for Cooking for pregnant women

In places all three types of note can be found. Example:

004.21   Systems analysis and design

Class communications network design and architecture in 004.65

For software systems analysis and design, see 005.12; for database design and architecture, see 005.74

See also 003 for Interdisciplinary works on systems analysis and design; also 658.4032 for Management use of systems analysis

Notes that explain changes or irregularities in the schedules and tables

'Discontinued' notes

These notes are used when a number or series of numbers have been discontinued completely, in which case concepts have usually been moved to a more general number, or when part of the contents of a number has been moved. Numbers that have been discontinued completely are enclosed in square brackets. Examples:

547[.79]   Nucleic acids

Number discontinued; class in 547.7

384[.352–.354]   Broadcast and interactive videotext

Numbers discontinued; class in 384.35

306.874   Parent–child relationship

Use of this number for youngest child discontinued; class in 306.87

Relocation notes

These notes are self-explanatory and explain any changes since the previous edition of DDC. Examples:

306 [.735] Cohabitation

Cohabitation relocated to 306.841; ménage a trois relocated to 306.8423

Then at 306.841 and 306.8423 respectively:

306.841   Cohabitation [*formerly* 306.735]

306.8423 Polygamy

Including menage a trois [*formerly* 306.735]

'Do not use' notes

Do not use notes relate to use of standard subdivisions. They instruct the classifier either to use standard subdivision at a broader number, or specify which part(s) of the standard subdivision the note relates to. Examples:

749.3   Specific kinds of furniture

[.301–309] Standard subdivisions

Do not use; class in 749.01–749.09

028   Reading and use of other information media

[.083]   Young people

Do not use; class in 028.5

In the second example above, –083 is the notation for young people in Table 1, standard subdivisions. The instruction here is not to use the standard subdivision for young people, as this aspect of the topic is deemed important enough to have its own number in the main schedules. Reading and use of other information media by persons in late adulthood, for example, does not have its own number in the schedules, so in this case the standard Subdivision *could* be added to the class number: 028.0846.

Instruction notes

In addition to the notes explained above, the schedules contain instructions for the classifier with regard to:

- number building;
- precedence order;
- options.

Notes that instruct the classifier in number building

Because DDC does not list absolutely everything in its schedules, classifiers must create notations for complex subjects by adding to a more general notation – thus numbers for complex subjects are built using the tables in volume 1, or built from numbers listed in other parts of the schedules. Number building using the tables is dealt with in detail below. In addition, there are many places in the schedules where the classifier is instructed to find a number elsewhere in the schedules and add it to the number at hand. Examples:

> 155.451–455   Exceptional children
>
>   Add to base number 155.45 the numbers following 371.9 in 371.91–371.95, e.g. psychology of gifted children 155.455

The schedules will always include an example of how number building is applied. If the classifier is unsure of how to proceed, then they should simply work through the example given. In the example above, the base number is 155.45; the classifier can then turn to the education schedules at 371.95 to discover what the second 5 in the example represents. At 371.95 we find: Gifted students. Now we can infer that the psychology of children with mental disabilities is 155.452 (155.45 plus the 2 from 371.92).

At times the classifier is instructed to add any notation from the schedules to achieve a subject-specific coverage. Example:

> 025.06001–06999 Information storage and retrieval systems for specific disciplines and subjects
>
>   Add to base number 025.06 notation 001–999, e.g. MEDLINE 025.0661

In this example, the base number is 025.06, MEDLINE is a database covering medicine and health, the DDC number for this discipline is 610, so the classifier simply adds 61 to specify the subject. NB: Any DDC number longer than three digits never ends with a zero, thus the zero from 610 is ignored. Applying this rule, we can create notations for other subject-specific retrieval tools:

PsycINFO 025.0615   (base number plus notation for psychology – 150)

LISA 025.0602   (base number plus notation for library science – 020)

Notes that prescribe preference order

These notes help the classifier to decide which aspect of the subject of a work should be used when it contains equal treatment of several topics. Example:

006   Special computer methods

> Unless other instructions are given, class a subject with aspects in two or more subdivisions of 006 in the number coming last, e.g. natural language processing in expert systems 006.35 (not 006.33)

In this example, the work would be classified at the number for natural language processing.

Sometimes the classifier is presented with a table of preference. Example:

155.9   Environmental psychology

> Unless other instructions are given, observe the following table of preference, e.g. the influence of family, friends and work associates upon persons coping with a loss through death 155.937 (not 155.92)

influence of specific situations	155.93
influence of clothing	155.95
influence of restrictive environments	155.96
influence of injuries, diseases, physical disabilities, disfigurements	155.916

influence of community and housing	155.94
influence of social environment	155.92
influence of physical environment and conditions (*except* 155.916)	155.91

So in this example the specific situation (loss through death) takes precedence over the social environment (family, friends and work associates).

When a single work deals with multiple aspects of a subject, e.g. age, gender and race, instructions are sometimes given in the schedules as to the order in which the aspects can be represented in a notation. So in this case the classifier is permitted to incorporate multiple aspects of a topic in the notation but must take care to follow prescribed citation order. If citation order is not given, then the classifier has to choose among the various aspects according to instructions for preference. It must be emphasised that it is important to always follow the instructions. For example, do not add one standard subdivision to another standard subdivision unless specifically instructed to in the schedules or tables. Example of citation order specified in the schedules:

330.9 Economic situation and conditions

.93–99 Geographical treatment by specific continents, countries, localities

Add to base number 330.9 notation 3–9 from Table 2, e.g. economic situation and conditions in France 330.944; then to the result add historical period numbers from appropriate subdivisions of 930–990, e.g. economic situation and conditions in France under Louis XIV 330.944033. In all cases use one 0 except 00 for North and South America, e.g. economic situation in the United States during reconstruction period 330.97308, in South America in 20th century 330.980033

This is a very complicated example and it is probably useful to work through the three examples given in the schedules.

The base number is, in every case, 330.9, now we add the area notation from Table 2:

France	–44
United States	–73
South America	–8

These notations can be added directly to the base number. Now we have economic situation and conditions in:

France	330.944
United States	330.973
South America	330.98

Now we add a single zero for the French and United States examples and two zeros for the South America example. Yes, the US is in North America, but the instructions to add two zeros only refer to works that cover all of either North or South America, not individual countries within those continents – this seems rather ambiguous but can be inferred from the example given. Next we turn to the history schedules:

French history, reign of Louis XIV	944.033
US history, reconstruction period	973.8
South American history, 20th century	980.033

Finally, we add those historical period numbers, ignoring the part of the number that is applied to all that country's history. For example, all periods of French history begin with 944.0, so we ignore that part of the notation and simply add 33 to specify the reign of Louis XIV. Thus:

$$330.9+44+0+33 = 330.944033$$
$$330.9+73+0+8\ \ = 330.97308$$
$$330.9+8+00+33 = 330.980033$$

Notes that explain options

These notes are in parentheses and are clearly labelled. They allow individual classifiers some flexibility in how works are classified. Having decided upon which option will best suit the needs of library users, that option should be applied in all cases. Examples:

016   Bibliographies and catalogues of works on specific subjects or in specific disciplines

(Option: class with the specific discipline or subject, using notation 016 from Table 1, e.g. bibliographies of medicine 610.16)

An individual library can elect to classify all subject bibliographies at 016, or can elect to classify them with their subject.

In the religion schedules, for example at 296.1, a whole series of optional numbers is provided. Each number is listed in round brackets and each has a note directing the classifier to a preferred number. Example:

296 (.1161) psalms (sources of Judaism) (optional number; prefer 222–224)

Depending on local needs a classifier can place psalms within Judaism or within Christianity under Poetic books of Old Testament at 223.2.

Number building using the tables

The tables, numbered 1–6 in volume 1 of DDC22, give the classifier a flexible tool with which to expand numbers listed in the schedules. Every number listed in the tables is preceded by a dash to show that it cannot be used on its own as a class number – the classifier does not include the dash when attaching one of these numbers to a notation.

Each table will be dealt with in turn, although it must be pointed out that some tables are only used very rarely, and only when specific instructions are found in the schedules. The most frequently used tables are 1 and 2 – standard subdivisions and geographical areas.

Table 1 Standard subdivisions

These are:

–01   Philosophy and theory

–02   Miscellany

–03   Dictionaries, encyclopaedias, concordances

–04   Special topics

–05   Serial publications

–06   Organisations and management

–07   Education, research, related topics

–08   History and description with respect to kinds of persons

–09   Historical, geographical, persons treatment

Unless specific instructions say otherwise, standard subdivisions can be used with any number. One example of where they cannot be used is for topics in standing room as explained previously.

Sometimes the standard subdivisions are printed in the schedules themselves. Example:

500 Natural sciences and mathematics

501 Philosophy and theory

502 Miscellany

503 Dictionaries, encyclopaedias, concordances

505 Serial publications

506 Organisations and management

507 Education, research, related topics

509 Historical, geographic, persons treatment

NB: The base number for science is 5 but it is represented in the schedules as 500 because no DDC number can be less than three digits long. As a standard subdivision is being added, the two zeros are ignored and the two-digit standard subdivisions are added to the base number 5.

The most common situation is where no instructions are given for adding standard subdivisions – in this case you can assume that they are added using a single zero. Examples:

305.520941   the British upper classes

Base number for the upper classes is 305.52; to this, we can add notation 09: historical, geographic, persons treatment from Table 1, and 41: British Isles from Table 2.

610.3   medical dictionaries

Base number for medicine is 61 (we can ignore the final zero as we are adding to the number); to this we add 03: dictionaries, encyclopedias, concordances from Table 1.

The exceptions to this rule are specified in the schedules. Some standard subdivisions are introduced by a double zero. Example:

652.3   Keyboarding

.3001–.3009   Standard subdivisions

A history of typing would be classified at 652.3009.

Some standard subdivisions are introduced by a triple zero. Example:

620   Engineering and allied operations

620.001–009 Standard subdivisions and engineering design and quality

An engineering dictionary would be classified at 620.003.

Table 2 Geographical areas, historical periods, persons

The basic arrangement is as follows:

–01–05 Historical periods (e.g. 20th century: 04)

–1 Areas, regions, places in general; oceans and seas

–2 Persons

–3 The ancient world

–4 Europe

–5 Asia, Orient, Far East

–6 Africa

–7 North America

–8 South America

–9 Other parts of the world and extra-terrestrial worlds

This is by far the longest of the tables and has undergone major revision in an attempt to keep up to date with political geography.

Very often a classifier might want to express in a notation that a work deals with a specific country or region. Example: a work on the incidence of tuberculosis in the developing world:

Incidence of tuberculosis	614.542
Developing regions (Table 2)	–1724
Incidence of tuberculosis in the developing world:	614.542091724

The tables allow for a lot of detail:

Incidence of tuberculosis in Europe 614.542094

Britain	614.5420941
England	614.5420942
London	614.54209421
Lambeth	614.5420942165

Where specific instructions are not given in the schedules, the classifier precedes the Table 2 notation with the 09 standard subdivision from Table 1 – historical, geographical, persons treatment – as in the above examples. Although a long notation is being created, it is actually very simple to construct – it is an easy rule to remember.

There are exceptions to this rule. In some cases, area notations can be added directly to schedule numbers. Example:

> 378.4–9 higher education in specific continents, countries, localities in modern world
>
> > Add to base number 378 notation 4–9 from Table 2, e.g. higher education in Mexico 378.72

Table 3 Subdivisions for the arts, for individual literatures, for specific literary forms

This is actually three tables:

3A   Subdivisions for works by or about individual authors

3B   Subdivisions for works by or about more than one author

3C   Notation to be added where instructed in Tables 3B, 700.4, 791.4, 808–809

The notations in Table 3 are only used following the instructions given under 700.4, 791.4 and 808–809, and following 810–890 in the schedules. Examples:

> Collected plays of Tennessee Williams: 812.5
>
> > base number for American literature in English: 81
> >
> > add notation for drama from Table 3A: –2
> >
> > add period number for 20th century from table at 810.1–818: 5
>
> German epic poetry: 831.032
>
> > base number for German literature: 83
> >
> > add notation for epic poetry from Table 3B: –1032
>
> Surrealism in the arts: 700.41163
>
> > arts displaying specific qualities of style, mood, viewpoint: 700.41

add the numbers following –1 in notation 11–18 from Table 3C: surrealism: –1163

add 163 to base number

Vampire films: 791.43675

films dealing with specific themes and subjects: 791.4362–4368

add the numbers following –3 in notation 32–38 from Table 3C: vampires: –375

add 75 to base number

Table 4 Subdivisions of individual languages and language families

Notations from this table are only used as instructed under 420–490. Examples:

Dutch grammar: 439.315

Dutch language: 439.31

add notation 1–8 from Table 4: grammar: –5

Welsh language dictionary: 491.663

Welsh language: 491.66

add notation 1–8 from Table 4: dictionaries: –3

English–Spanish phrasebook: 468.3421 (assume Spanish for English speakers)

base number for Spanish language: 46

add notation 1–8 from Table 4: audio-lingual approach to expression for persons whose native language is different: –834

add notation 2–9 from Table 6: English language: –21

Table 5 Ethnic and national groups

Notations in this table are added according to instructions in the schedules, or preceded by the standard subdivision –089 (ethnic and national groups) from Table 1. So they are added following the same rules as area notations from Table 2 which were preceded by 09. Examples:

Chinese Americans: 305.8951073

> base number for specific ethnic and national (social) groups: 305.8

> add notation 5–9 from Table 5: Chinese: –951

> add 0 and then add notation 3–9 from Table 2 for area in which a group is located: United States: –73

Inuit death customs: 393.0899712

> death customs: 393

> add notation for ethnic and national groups from Table 1: –089

> add notation 5–9 from Table 5: North American native peoples: –97

> add numbers following –97 in notation 971–979 from Table 6: Inuit: –12

Table 6 Languages

Notations from Table 6 are again added as instructed in the schedules or other tables (as in previous examples). Example:

The Bible in French: 220.541

> base number for versions of the bible in other languages: 220.5

> add notation 3–9 from Table 6: French language: 41

Notation

In Chapter 1, we examined the qualities that notation should possess. These will now be examined and evaluated with specific reference to DDC.

Notation must convey order

Probably one reason why DDC is so popular is that its notation is very easy to follow. It is an example of a pure notation, using only Arabic numerals, and so there can be no confusion about which type of symbol is cited first and we recognise that 150 comes before 152. However, not everyone is comfortable with decimal fractions. Personal experience confirms that some library users are confused about the order after the decimal point – thinking that 152.14 comes after 152.8, for example (translating the .14 as fourteen).

The notation should be brief and simple

Brevity and simplicity have obvious advantages. Brief and simple notations are more easily memorised and recalled, and re-shelving of materials and shelf tidying is easier. DDC achieves simplicity through its use of a pure notation with self-evident order. Brevity of notation is, however, variable. Often the only way to keep the notation brief is to sacrifice detail and classify subjects more broadly. Some libraries may decide to instigate a policy that no notations should exceed 12 numbers, for example. This may entail omitting the geographical area code. For most general collections it could be argued that simplicity and brevity are more important than depth of classification.

In parts of the DDC schedules, in subject areas that have undergone rapid expansion, brevity has clearly suffered. The best evidence for this can be found in the engineering schedules. Examples:

Television maintenance and repair:	621.38800288
Turboprop engines:	629.1343532

Works on industrial economics often generate particularly lengthy notations. The base numbers, for example 338.45 and 338.47, can have any number in the schedules added to them to specify particular industries. Examples:

Production efficiency in semiconductor industries:	338.4562138832
production efficiency:	338.45
semiconductors:	621.38832
Teddy bear manufacturing industries:	338.476887243
services and specific products:	338.47
teddy bear manufacture:	688.7243

These notations could, of course, be added to further:

Production efficiency in semiconductor industries in the United States: 338.45621388320973

Add to base number 09 from Table 1 to indicate geographic treatment, then add 73 from Table 2 to specify United States.

Teddy bear manufacturing industries in postwar Germany: 338.476887243094309045

Add to base number 09 from Table 1 to indicate geographic treatment, then add 43 from Table 2 to specify Germany, then add 09 from Table 1 to indicate historical treatment, then add 045 to specify postwar period.

The notation should be memorable

Systematic mnemonics is the main type of memory aid used in DDC. There are many instances where the same symbol or group of symbols is always used to denote the same subject concept. The clearest examples of DDC's use of systematic mnemonics can be found in the language, literature and history schedules and in the geographic areas, ethnic and national groups and languages tables. Example:

Italian language	450
Italian literature	850
Italian history	945
Italy	45 (Table 2)
Italian people	51 (Table 5)
Italian language	5 (Table 6)

Thus, 5 represents Italy or Italian. Likewise 2 represents English, 3 represents German, 4 represents French, and so on. However, as we have already noted in Chapter 1, DDC's use of systematic mnemonics is not entirely consistent. For example, 03 is the standard subdivision (Table 1) for a dictionary or encyclopaedia, but in places two or more zeros are required when adding standard subdivisions:

dictionary of biology:	570.3
dictionary of physics:	530.03
dictionary of engineering:	620.003

The notation should be hospitable to the insertion of new subjects

As well as being able to accommodate new subjects, it is important that new subjects are accommodated in their correct place within the classification scheme, the place that shows their relationship to existing subjects. There are three ways in which DDC achieves hospitality:

1. Decimal notation – a new subject can be fitted almost anywhere in a sequence by using decimal subdivision. Example: 621 applied physics

621.1	Steam engineering
621.2	Hydraulic-power technology
621.3	Electrical, magnetic, optical, communications, computer engineering; electronics, lighting
621.38	Electronics, communications engineering
621.388	Television
621.38833	Video recorders and video recordings
621.4	Prime movers and heat engineering

   It is clear from this example that brevity of notation has suffered. The subject of electrical engineering has grown enormously, and the only way new subjects could be added was to add numbers after the decimal point. Helpful order of subjects can also be argued to be lacking in this part of the DDC schedules – with technologies like television and computers coming between hydraulic technologies such as water mills and heat engineering which includes nuclear reactors.

2. Unassigned notation – leave gaps into which new subjects can be fitted. Of course, this approach is not always satisfactory because gaps might not be in the right places. It is very difficult to predict the areas in which new subjects are likely to arise. Computing is an excellent example of how DDC can accommodate new subjects, but at the expense of helpful order. Dewey could not have foreseen computing when he originally devised his scheme in the 1870s and as the subject started to emerge in the twentieth century it was accommodated (reasonably) successfully in the mathematics and engineering schedules: at 510.78 in DDC16 (1958) and in 510.78 and 621.38195 in DDC17 (1965). In DDC18 (1971) computing was moved into the generalities main class, at 001.65, with technical aspects remaining in 621.38195. The discipline grew very rapidly throughout the 1970s and the 1980s and in DDC20 (1989) computing had been moved again to 004–006, the probable reason being that this was the largest gap in the schedules. In DDC22 the generalities class has been renamed 'computer science, information, general works', so, in effect, computing has been awarded main class status. Computing's location certainly does not

reflect its relationship to other subjects, but the ability of DDC to accommodate large and rapidly developing new subject areas demonstrates the scheme's hospitality.

3. Include 'other' classes – create classes with non-specific titles to accommodate any subjects that may have been omitted when the scheme was first devised. These are found throughout the DDC schedules. Examples:

290   Other religions

490   Other languages

629   Other branches of engineering

890   Literatures of other languages

990   History of other areas

Apart from being a useful device to accommodate unforeseen subjects, use of an 'other' class is an inevitable consequence of Dewey's insistence on decimal structure – not every subject can be neatly divided into groups of ten.

The 'other branches of engineering' example is interesting as it demonstrates how helpful order of classes can suffer as new subjects are accommodated.

620   Engineering and allied operations

621   Applied physics

622   Mining and related operations

623   Military and nautical engineering

624   Civil engineering

625   Engineering of railroads and roads

[626]   [unassigned]

627   Hydraulic engineering

628   Sanitary and municipal engineering; environmental protection engineering

629   Other branches of engineering

The 629 class is where transportation engineering is located, together with automatic control engineering (automatons). This seems especially curious as the 626 class is vacant and it would seem to be more logical to have engineering of vehicles adjacent to rail and road engineering. Location within an 'other' class does not adequately represent transportation engineering's relationship with other branches of engineering nor its status as a subject – is it less important than hydraulic or sanitary engineering, for example?

Notation might show hierarchy: expressiveness

This is a quality one would expect to find in an enumerative classification scheme. DDC's rigid structure should provide an ideal framework within which to develop expressive notation. Generally DDC displays hierarchical relationships between subjects quite well and provides for a shelf arrangement that promotes browsing. Example:

344.046	Environmental protection law
344.0462	Wastes
344.04622	Kinds of waste
344.04626	Disposal into specific environments
344.0463	Pollution and noise
344.04632	Pollution
344.04633	Pollutants
344.046332	Oil
344.046334	Pesticides
344.046335	Asbestos
344.046336	Acid rain
344.04634	Pollution of specific environments
344.046342	Air pollution
344.046343	Water pollution
344.04638	Noise
344.0464	Sanitation in places of public assembly
344.0465	Industrial sanitation and safety

This example shows a beautifully structured hierarchy. Subjects have clear relationships and their expression moves logically from the general to the specific and vice versa. This is taken from a part of the schedules that has been revised in the new edition and shows significant improvement from DDC21's expression of this subject area.

However, expressiveness can suffer when new subjects are added and/or number building is applied. This is a problem that is not intrinsic to DDC; rather it is in the nature of hierarchies to start to break down as they grow in size and complexity. Example:

354	Public administration of economy and environment
354.9	Administration of labour and professions
354.94	Labour in specific extractive, manufacturing, construction occupations
354.9422334	Administration of labour in the coal mining industry

The final notation here represents a number built by adding the notation (without the initial number 6) for specific industries from the 620–690 part of the schedules. Allowing the classifier to build notations in this way avoids duplication of concepts in the listing of subjects, but expressiveness is inevitably lost.

It is possible to find many examples of hierarchical decay in the DDC schedules but this is inevitable and so cannot be considered a major criticism of the scheme. If a classification scheme is to be hospitable to the accommodation of new subjects, then expressiveness must be sacrificed.

The notation should allow for flexibility

Given Dewey's rigid structure, it is not surprising that flexibility is somewhat lacking. It is essential that classifiers adhere to the rules for representation of subjects and for number building as laid down in the schedules. Unlike in Universal Decimal Classification, for example, it is not possible to build numbers for composite subjects by combining existing notations, unless the schedules have explicit instructions to that effect. However, there is some provision for flexibility. In these instances a preferred order is given together with an option or options, often with a reference to the manual. For example:

920.1–928   Biography of specific classes of persons

Option A: use subdivisions identified by *

Option B: class individual biography in 92 or B; class collected biography in 92 or 920 undivided

Option C: class individual biography of men in 920.71; class individual biography of women in 920.72

(Prefer specific discipline or subject, plus notation 092 from Table 1, e.g. collected biography of scientists 509.22)

Obviously it is essential to be consistent when using options. If a decision is made to class subject-specific biographies with the subject, then that rule must be applied consistently and without exception.

Overview

Like any classification scheme that aspires to cover all knowledge, DDC has its faults. Coverage in some areas like religion demonstrates an antiquated bias reflecting the cultural context within which the scheme was created. Class numbers can be very lengthy, even for quite simple topics. Its rigid structure and preponderance of rules can seem overly restrictive at times. Newer disciplines like computing and electrical engineering have not been accommodated very successfully. interdisciplinary topics like women's studies and media studies are unhelpfully dispersed across the schedules (and across the library shelves).

Nevertheless, DDC is deservedly a very widely used classification scheme in public and academic libraries. In general, it provides a well structured and helpful arrangement of materials on the library shelves. It is a very familiar scheme, and one that is quite easy to grasp for the library user. Its hospitality can be criticised, but new subjects are accommodated. Regular revisions of the hard-copy version and access to the very latest changes to the scheme via WebDewey ensure that the scheme keeps pace with new areas of knowledge.

Recommended reading

Dewey Decimal Classification (2003) 22nd edn. Dublin, OH: OCLC.
Foskett, A.C. (1996) Chapter 17 in *The Subject Approach to Information*, 5th edn. London: Library Association.

The DDC schedules themselves are the best source of information about the scheme. In volume 1, an excellent background and introduction to the scheme are provided together with instructions on its use. The OCLC website at *http://www.oclc.org* includes detailed documentation and online training as well as the electronic version of the scheme.

Foskett provides good analytical coverage of DDC's structure and use, but examples are taken from the 20th edition. Other published guides to the use of the scheme also deal with earlier editions and so will provide basic background but examples may be out of date. An example of a text with coverage of the 21st edition is:

Chan, L.M et al. (1996) *Dewey Decimal Classification: A Practical Guide*. Albany, NY: Forest Press.

Practical exercises

Completing the practical exercises will allow you to familiarise your-selves with the structure of the DDC schedules and to gain experience in number building. It is strongly recommended that the hard-copy version of the scheme is used rather than the electronic version. Use of the hard-copy will help new classifiers to become familiar with the structure of the scheme as a whole. (Answers are given in the Appendix at the end of the book.)

In DDC22, what subjects do the following notations represent?

070.5797

973.3115

133.3337

248.8431

681.145

621.388337

551.461364

338.4766342

822.3

372.72044

614.534

398.24529773

025.52774

305.4302092

427.88

639.3757

599.361565

785.7194

Using DDC22, classify the following:

Human physiology

Animal behaviour

Visual perception

Encyclopaedia of medicine

Neurophysiology

Book of Common Prayer

German grammar

How to play bridge

Education of gifted children

Winter cookery

Research methods in organic chemistry

The Koran (English translation)

Word for Windows manual

History of the trade union movement

Ethics of human cloning

The Prelude by William Wordsworth (*Wordsworth was an English Romantic poet*)

Information retrieval systems in pharmacology

Richard Feynman: a biography (*Feynman was a physicist*)

Drug treatment of Parkinson's disease

Howard Hodgkin: paintings (*Hodgkin is an English artist*)

Nurse education in the United States

Statistical methods in psychology

Fashion in Restoration England

Films of Orson Welles (*Welles as a film director*)

Library of Congress Classification

Background

The development of the Library of Congress Classification (LCC) can be traced back to 1897, with the first schedule, History: America published in 1901. The scheme evolved over many years, with schedules for separate subject areas being published after 1901 (the first Law schedule was not published until 1969) (Chan, 1999). There are, at the time of writing, 47 separate schedules, and unfortunately no printed index providing overall coverage. Libraries using or wishing to use LCC should subscribe to the electronic version available via the Library of Congress website (*http://www.loc.gov*). The electronic version is constantly revised and updated and its use dispenses with the need to store bulky print versions of the scheme (a single schedule can be over 300 pages in length).

Unlike other schemes LCC is not based on theories of classification or the organisation of knowledge. It was devised as a practical tool to classify the US National Library collection and was not originally intended to be adopted by other libraries. As a consequence of its purely practical purpose, no attempt was made to create an elegant or logical structure. LCC is not so much an embodiment of knowledge, more a detailed topic listing. This means that, unlike in the case of DDC, there is no advantage to be gained from learning the structure of the scheme by using the print version.

Coverage

LCC has, as you might imagine given its size, a very detailed listing of subjects. Inevitably there is a distinct bias towards the US in its coverage of subjects – a very good reason why it has not been as widely adopted as DDC outside the US.

Library of Congress Classification: outline

A   General works

AC   Collections. Series. Collected works

AE   Encyclopedias

AG   Dictionaries and other general reference works

AI   Indexes

AM   Museums. Collectors and collecting

AN   Newspapers

AP   Periodicals

AS   Academies and learned societies

AY   Yearbooks. Almanacs. Directories

AZ   History of scholarship and learning. The humanities

B   **Philosophy. Psychology. Religion**

B   Philosophy (general)

BC   Logic

BD   Speculative philosophy

BF   Psychology

BH   Aesthetics

BJ   Ethics

BL   Religions. Mythology. Rationalism

BM   Judaism

BP   Islam. Bahaism. Theosophy, etc.

BQ   Buddhism

BR   Christianity

BS   The Bible

BT   Doctrinal theology

BV   Practical theology

BX   Christian denominations

C   **Auxiliary sciences of history**

C   Auxiliary sciences of history (general)

CB   History of civilisation

CC   Archaeology

CD   Diplomatics. Archives. Seals

CE   Technical chronology. Calendar

CJ   Numismatics

CN   Inscriptions. Epigraphy

CR   Heraldry

CS   Genealogy

CT   Biography

D   **History (general) and history of Europe**

D   History (general)

DA   Great Britain

DAW Central Europe

DB   Austria – Liechtenstein – Hungary – Czechoslovakia

DC   France – Andorra – Monaco

DD   Germany

DE   Greco-Roman world

DF   Greece

DG   Italy – Malta

DH   Low Countries – Benelux countries

DJ   Netherlands (Holland)

DJK   Eastern Europe (general)

DK   Russia. Soviet Union. Former Soviet republics – Poland

DL   Northern Europe. Scandinavia

DP   Spain – Portugal

DQ   Switzerland

DR   Balkan Peninsula

DS   Asia

DT   Africa

DU   Oceania (South Seas)

DX   Gypsies

E–F   **History: America**

E	11–143	America
	151–889	United States
F	1–975	United States local history
	1001–1145.2	British America (including Canada) Dutch America

1170	French America
1201–3799	Latin America. Spanish America

G   Geography. Anthropology. Recreation

G   Geography (general). Atlases. Maps

GA   Mathematical geography. Cartography

GB   Physical geography

GC   Oceanography

GE   Environmental sciences

GF   Human ecology. Anthropogeography

GN   Anthropology

GR   Folklore

GT   Manners and customs (general)

GV   Recreation. Leisure

H   Social sciences

H   Social sciences (general)

HA   Statistics

HB   Economic theory. Demography

HC   Economic history and conditions

HD   Industries. Land use. Labour

HE   Transportation and communications

HF   Commerce

HG   Finance

HJ   Public finance

HM   Sociology (general)

HN   Social history and conditions. Social problems. Social reform

HQ   The family. Marriage. Women

HS   Societies: secret, benevolent, etc.

HT   Communities. Classes. Races

HV   Social pathology. Social and public welfare. Criminology

HX   Socialism. Communism. Anarchism

J   Political science

J   General legislative and executive papers

JA   Political science (general)

JC   Political theory

JF   Political institutions and public administration – general

JJ   Political institutions and public administration – North America

JK   Political institutions and public administration – United States

JL   Political institutions and public administration – Canada, West Indies, Mexico, Central and South America

JN   Political institutions and public administration – Europe

JQ   Political institutions and public administration – Asia, Arab countries, Islamic countries, Africa, Atlantic Ocean islands, Australia, New Zealand, Pacific Ocean islands

JS   Local government. Municipal government

JV   Colonies and colonisation. Emigration and immigration. International migration

JX   International law – see KZ (notation obsolete)

JZ   International relations

K   Law

K   Law in general. Comparative and uniform law. Jurisprudence

KBM   Jewish law

KBP   Islamic law

KBR   History of canon law

KBU   Law of the Roman Catholic church. The Holy See

KD–KDK   United Kingdom and Ireland

KDZ   America. North America

KE   Canada

KF   United States

KG   Latin America – Mexico and Central America – West Indies. Caribbean area

KH   South America

KJ–KKZ Europe

KL–KWX Asia and Eurasia, Africa, Pacific area and Antarctica

KZ   Law of nations

L   Education

L   Education (general)

LA   History of education

LB   Theory and practice of education

LC   Special aspects of education

LD   Individual institutions – United States

LE   Individual institutions – America (except United States)

LF   Individual institutions – Europe

LG   Individual institutions – Asia, Africa, Indian Ocean islands, Australia, New Zealand, Pacific islands

LH   College and school magazines and papers

LJ   Student fraternities and societies, United States

LT   Textbooks

M   Music and books on music

M   Music

ML   Literature on music

MT   Musical instruction and study

N   Fine arts

N   Visual arts

NA   Architecture

NB   Sculpture

NC   Drawing. Design. Illustration

ND   Painting

NE   Print media

NK   Decorative arts

NX   Arts in general

P   **Language and literature**

P   Philology. Linguistics

PA   Greek language and literature. Latin language and literature

PB   Modern languages. Celtic languages

PC   Romanic languages

PD   Germanic languages. Scandinavian languages

PE   English language

PF   West Germanic languages

PG   Slavic languages. Baltic languages. Albanian language

PH   Uralic languages. Basque language

PJ   Oriental languages and literatures

PK   Indo-Iranian languages and literatures

PL   Languages and literatures of Eastern Asia, Africa, Oceania

PM   Hyperborean, Indian and artificial languages

PN   Literature (general)

PQ   French literature – Italian literature – Spanish literature – Portuguese literature

PR   English literature

PS   American literature

PT   German literature – Dutch literature – Flemish literature since 1830 – Afrikaans literature – Scandinavian literature – Old Norse literature: Old Icelandic and Old Norwegian – modern Icelandic literature – Faroese literature – Danish literature – Norwegian literature – Swedish literature

PZ   Fiction and juvenile belles lettres

Q   **Science**

Q   Science (general)

QA   Mathematics

QB   Astronomy

QC   Physics

QD   Chemistry

QE   Geology

QH Natural history – biology

QK Botany

QL Zoology

QM Human anatomy

QP Physiology

QR Microbiology

R Medicine

R Medicine (general)

RA Public aspects of medicine

RB Pathology

RC Internal medicine

RD Surgery

RE Ophthalmology

RF Otorhinolaryngology

RG Gynaecology and obstetrics

RJ Paediatrics

RK Dentistry

RL Dermatology

RM Therapeutics. Pharmacology

RS Pharmacy and materia medica

RT Nursing

RV Botanic, Thomsonian and eclectic medicine

RX Homeopathy

RZ Other systems of medicine

S Agriculture

S Agriculture (general)

SB Plant culture

SD Forestry

SF Animal culture

SH Aquaculture. Fisheries. Angling

SK Hunting sports

T	Technology
T	Technology (general)
TA	Engineering (general). Civil engineering
TC	Hydraulic engineering. Ocean engineering
TD	Environmental technology. Sanitary engineering
TE	Highway engineering. Roads and pavements
TF	Railroad engineering and operation
TG	Bridge engineering
TH	Building construction
TJ	Mechanical engineering and machinery
TK	Electrical engineering. Electronics. Nuclear engineering
TL	Motor vehicles. Aeronautics. Astronautics
TN	Mining engineering. Metallurgy
TP	Chemical technology
TR	Photography
TS	Manufactures
TT	Handicrafts. Arts and crafts
TX	Home economics

U	Military science
U	Military science (general)
UA	Armies: organisation, distribution, military situation
UB	Military administration
UC	Maintenance and transportation
UD	Infantry
UE	Cavalry. Armour
UF	Artillery
UG	Military engineering. Air forces
UH	Other services

V	Naval science
V	Naval science (general)
VA	Navies: organisation, distribution, naval situation

VB   Naval administration

VC   Naval maintenance

VD   Naval seamen

VE   Marines

VF   Naval ordnance

VG   Minor services of navies

VK   Navigation. Merchant marine

VM   Naval architecture. Shipbuilding. Marine engineering

Z   **Bibliography, library science, information resources (general)**

Z   Books (general). Writing. Palaeography. Book industries and trade. Libraries. Bibliography

ZA   Information resources (general)

Structure and use

As can be seen in the outline of the scheme, there is nothing systematic about the ordering of the main classes. Apparent anomalies can be identified throughout the schedules. For example:

- It seems odd that the HX topics appear in social rather than political science – an explanation may be that the political schedules seem to have an emphasis on practice rather than theory.

- It is interesting to note that in the law schedules the UK and Ireland are separated from Europe, especially as our legal systems are obviously increasingly influenced by EU law.

- The science schedules have a similar arrangement to Dewey Decimal Classification, Universal Decimal Classification and Bliss Bibliographic Classification, and it is pleasing to have some consensus about organisation of topics within a class. However, microbiology has been added to the listing of subjects after aspects of plant, animal and human biology, there has been no attempt (unlike in DDC) to accommodate it within the biological sciences.

- It is not clear why angling and hunting are in the agriculture schedules – these topics are in the recreation schedules in DDC, and certainly the terms *angling and hunting sports* suggest 'recreational' activities.

- There appears to be some inconsistent attempt at mnemonics – M for music, T for technology, and so on, but the use of mnemonics is very patchy.

Certainly anomalies like those described above and the lack of a logical structure offend the classification theorist. Nevertheless, LCC is an exceptionally popular scheme and is second only to DDC in its adoption. Its main advantage is that it is relatively easy to use because the listing of subjects is very detailed which, to a large extent, dispenses with the need to build notations. For example, in DDC specific countries are specified by adding a geographic area notation from Table 2; in LCC individual countries were often enumerated in each part of the schedule that required a geographic treatment:

Railways in Namibia:	HE3432.3
Railways in Angola:	HE3433

Also, in the economic treatment of individual industries and trades, each industry or trade was enumerated:

Economic aspects of the urinary incontinence products industry:	HD9995.U74
Economic aspects of the barbers' supplies industry:	HD9999.B14

Recently, however, there has been a move to increasing use of tables in each schedule to list concepts that occur over several topics.

LCC's main disadvantage is probably that the listing is based on LC acquisitions and so completely new subjects can only be accommodated post publication. DDC takes a more generic approach and so is better able to anticipate and accommodate new areas of knowledge. For example, works on human cloning could be accommodated in DDC under genetic engineering at 660.65, or in medical ethics at 174.2, or in ethics of sex and reproduction at 176 before the subject name was specified. In LCC a classmark had to be assigned to the topic at QH442.2, which accommodates both the technical and ethical aspects of the subject. DDC has a greater degree of flexibility in its more generic approach to knowledge.

Notes

As in DDC, the notes in the LCC schedules provide essential information for the classifier. There are five main types of notes used in LCC:

- scope notes;
- see notes;
- including notes;
- confer notes;
- table notes.

Each of these is explained in detail below. In some cases Chan (1999) has been used to provide examples.

'Scope' notes

Scope notes in LCC explain what types of work are to be classified at a particular notation and are introduced by the words *class here*. Examples:

Genetics (in class QH)

Class here general and experimental works in genetics

Children. Child development (in class HQ)

Class here comprehensive works on child development which emphasize social growth of the child

Inorganic chemistry: special elements (QD181)

Class here works on the origin, properties, preparation, reactions, isotopes, and analytical chemistry of individual elements and their inorganic compounds

'See' notes

See notes in LCC are often used with scope notes to lead the classifier to a notation for other aspects of the topic. Example:

Children. Child development (in class HQ). *Following the scope note above*:

For works on child development which stress mainly the child's physical and psychological growth, see RJ131

When this type of see note is used alone, it is called an *explanatory* see note. Example:

Human anatomy: vascular system (QM178)

For works on the blood vessels of a particular organ or system, see the organ or system

This type of see note has replaced *prefer notes* (now discontinued) which previously performed the same function.

A third type of see note indicates relocation of a topic. Here the number is always enclosed in parentheses. Example:

QA Mathematics

(145) Arithmetic and algebra, see QA101–107

'Including' notes

Including notes are used to list the topics that are classified at a particular notation. Example:

SB Plant culture and horticulture

481 Parks and public reservations

Including theory, management, history

'Confer' notes

Confer notes act like related term or see also notes in that they indicate that related topics are found elsewhere in the schedules. Example:

QA Mathematics

911 Fluid dynamics. Hydrodynamics

Cf. TC160–181, hydraulics

Table notes

Table notes appear at points in the schedules where topics are not fully enumerated, as is increasingly the case. They refer to tables in the same schedule or same part of the schedule and are simply a space-saving device. These notes largely replace *divided like* notes that were found in older versions of the schedules. Example:

TK Electrical engineering. Electronics. Nuclear engineering

1221–1327 Power plants utilising heat energy (table T1)

Add country number in table to TK1200

Cutter numbers

Cutter numbers are named after Charles Ammi Cutter whose expansive classification was used as a guide in the development of LCC. In LCC Cutter numbers are used to identify individual authors and titles and also to indicate geographic areas and special topics. Cutter numbers help to ensure that a call number for any work is unique and they help to maintain an alphabetical arrangement. Cutter numbers are always preceded by a decimal point in the call number, and they consist of an initial letter followed by a number derived from the second and subsequent letters of the word. Cutter numbers are devised using Table 2.1.

There are also special tables of Cutter numbers. For example, there are over 100,000 geographic Cutter numbers in special tables that can be downloaded from the Library of Congress website as a PDF file.

Table 2.1   Cutter table

1. After initial vowels								
for the second letter	b	d	l–m	n	p	r	s–t	u–y
use number	2	3	4	5	6	7	8	9
2. After initial letter S								
for the second letter	a	ch	e	h–i	m–p	t	u	w–z
use number	2	3	4	5	6	7	8	9
3. After initial letters Qu								
for the second letter	a	e	i	o	r	t	y	
use number	3	4	5	6	7	8	9	
for initial letters Qa–Qt use 2–29								
4. After other initial consonants								
for the second letter	a	e	i	o	r	u	y	
use number	3	4	5	6	7	8	9	
5. For expansion								
for the letter	a–d	e–h	i–l	m–o	p–s	t–v	w–z	
use number	3	4	5	6	7	8	9	

Examples of authors' Cutter numbers using the Cutter table:

Auden	A93	Eliot	E45
Belloc	B45	Foskett	F67
Chrisite	C47	Unwin	U59
Scott	S36	McGuinness	M34
Twain	T93	Stewart	S74
Quick	Q53	White	W55

Where a number is not specified for a particular letter, then the number preceding or following that letter should be used (see the Scott and White examples). The point is that each author should have a unique Cutter number to maintain shelf order so numbers may need to be amended or extended to prevent duplication.

LCC call numbers

The LCC classmark or 'call number' is made up of two main parts, the class number and the book number.

The class number consists of:

- the letter(s) identifying the main class;
- the number(s) identifying the subclass;
- the decimal extension (if one exists);
- the Cutter number specified in the schedules (if one exists).

The book number consists of:

- the Cutter number for the main entry (author or title);
- the year of publication.

Examples:

Chan, L.M. (1999) A Guide to the Library of Congress Classification, 5th edn. Libraries Unlimited.

Z696.U4.C53 1999

Z   bibliography and library science

696   classification

U4	Cutter number (based on United States) for LCC (from internal table)
C53	Cutter number for Chan
1999	date of publication

Hendee, W.R. and Wells, P.T. (eds) (1997) *The Perception of Visual Information*, 2nd edn. Heidelberg: Springer.

QP475.P47 1997

QP	Physiology
475	Vision, general works
P47	Cutter number for 'perception' (main entry under title for edited works)
1997	Date of publication

Gupta, J.N.D. et al. (2004) *Creating Knowledge-Based Organizations*. Idea Group Publishing.

HD53.C74 2004

HD	Management
53	Intellectual work
C74	Cutter number for 'creating' (main entry under title for works by multiple authors)
2004	Date of publication

Call numbers are quite complex, but are simple to construct and provide an elegant means of uniquely identifying each item in the collection. The shelf order is alphabetical then numerical to establish a helpful order for main and subclasses, then Cutter numbers establish an alphanumeric order for individual authors/titles and the date ensures that items with the same author/title are shelved chronologically.

Notation

The notation must convey order

LCC uses a mixed notation – main classes and their major sections are represented by letters, with Arabic numerals used to represent divisions within those classes and sections. As in DDC numbers can be extended using the decimal point. Certainly the scheme has a self-evident order, alphanumeric, but notations are arguably less elegant than those derived from DDC's pure notation.

The notation should be brief and simple

Brevity is aided by use of letters rather than numbers for main classes and their major sections – a base of 26 rather than 10. LCC has 18 identifiable main classes and 230 major sections, most of which can be expressed by two letters. However, simplicity and brevity are lost because of the level of detail achieved in the schedules.

As we saw in the examples of call numbers above, LCC's use of integers, often of four figures, plus numbers after the decimal point, plus Cutter numbers can create long and complex notations that can increase time needed for shelving and shelf-tidying.

The notation should be memorable

There is a lot of evidence of literal mnemonics in class A: general works:

A   General works

AC   Collections. Series. Collected works

AE   Encyclopedias

AG   Dictionaries and other general reference works

AI   Indexes

AM   Museums. Collectors and collecting

AN   Newspapers

AP   Periodicals

AS   Academies and learned societies

AY   Yearbooks. Almanacs. Directories

AZ   History of scholarship and learning. The humanities

A problem is that this device is not applied consistently throughout the schedules.

There is little evidence of use of systematic mnemonics in the LCC schedules, but their use is likely to increase as more common concepts are listed in tables rather than enumerated fully throughout the schedules. One example of use of systematic mnemonics is that notations derived from the Cutter table are used to represent countries and states if an alphabetical arrangement is needed. Their use has not always been consistent, however. For example, in the table of regions and countries printed in the H schedules, Sri Lanka is represented by .S72, but where a country-by-country treatment had been enumerated in the schedules this notation may not have been used. For example: Railways in Sri Lanka: HE3300.3. The situation has now improved with more use of tables and less enumeration in the schedules.

As LCC is published in so many volumes it is difficult to get a sense of cohesion across subjects or disciplines. It can be claimed that the Cutter table utilises systematic mnemonics in its representations of authors' and other names.

The notation must be hospitable to the insertion of new subjects

An enumerative scheme, particularly one that lists concepts to the level of detail achieved in LCC, will have problems accommodating new topics. LCC utilises a very pragmatic approach in solving this problem: it does not have a hierarchical structure and does not aim for a helpful order of subjects, so new topics can be added very easily without compromising the overall structure of the scheme.

A very good test of hospitality is to examine where the discipline of computing or computer science has been accommodated. LCC has succeeded in accommodating computing in the science schedules within mathematics (QA) and in the technology schedules within electrical engineering (TK). As has already been explored, in DDC computing had to be moved from mathematics and electrical engineering as the discipline grew in size. LCC's greater hospitality allows the discipline to grow without the need to move it to a larger gap in the schedules.

The notation might show hierarchy: expressiveness

As noted above, when LCC was devised, a decision was made to sacrifice expressiveness to achieve a greater degree of brevity and hospitality. This is very sensible, particularly as the scheme was created to organise a national collection, most of which was not open access. However, when the scheme is applied to smaller library collections, the reduced capabilities for browsing can be a drawback.

The notation should allow for flexibility

LCC can certainly be criticised for its lack of flexibility, but this is inevitable in such a detailed enumerative classification scheme. To its credit LCC has attempted to increase its flexibility in answer to criticism (Chan, 1999). All subject bibliographies are classified within class Z, but alternative notations are now provided for libraries wishing to shelve subject bibliographies with their subject. For example, the preferred classmark for a bibliography of architecture is Z5943; an alternative location would be at NA2750.

Overview

Very detailed enumeration of subjects makes LCC a good choice for large academic libraries. It lacks many of the qualities demanded by classification theory, but in its pragmatic approach to problems of library organisation it succeeds in providing good coverage and excellent hospitality. Its lack of an expressive structure does not encourage browsing, which may be seen as a drawback by many users. Its notations are rather long and complicated through use of both letters and numbers and very detailed identification of individual authors and texts. Its major fault is perhaps that it is tied to the holdings of the Library of Congress, so publications dealing with new areas of knowledge have to be acquired by the Library of Congress before a classmark is allocated. Access to the electronic version of the scheme via the *http://www.loc.gov* website offers the availability of regular revisions and largely dispenses with the need to consult bulky hard-copy versions of the schedules.

Reference and recommended reading

Chan, L.M. (1999) *A Guide to the Library of Congress Classification*, 5th edn. Englewood, CO: Libraries Unlimited.
Dittmann, H. and Hardy, J. (2000) *Learn Library of Congress Classification*. London: Scarecrow.

Chan's book is extremely detailed and provides excellent background information as well as full coverage of each of the schedules of the scheme. It is highly recommended for readers wishing to gain an in-depth appreciation of LCC. Dittmann and Hardy's text provides a much more basic and practical approach and is recommended as a text for beginners.

Practical exercises

Here only the class and alphanumeric subclass notations are required, except where the Cutter number has been specifically requested. (Answers are given in the Appendix at the end of the book.)

Using LCC, classify the following

Human physiology

Animal behaviour

Visual perception

Encyclopaedia of medicine

Neurophysiology

Book of Common Prayer

German grammar

How to play bridge

Education of gifted children

Winter cookery

Research methods in organic chemistry

The Koran (English translation)

Word for Windows manual

History of the trade union movement

Ethics of human cloning

The Prelude by William Wordsworth (*Wordsworth was an English Romantic poet*)

Information retrieval systems in pharmacology

Richard Feynman: a biography (*Feynman was a physicist*)

Drug treatment of Parkinson's disease

Howard Hodgkin: paintings (*Hodgkin is an English artist*)

Nurse education in the United States

Statistical methods in psychology

Fashion in Restoration England

Films of Orson Welles (*Welles as a film director*)

3

Classification schemes for specialist collections

Universal Decimal Classification

Background

Universal Decimal Classification (UDC) is, at first glance, very similar to Dewey, from which it was developed. The original purpose was to use a modified and expanded version of DDC to organise a universal bibliography of everything that had been written throughout history (McIlwaine, 2000: 1). Thus its original purpose was for documentation, not shelf arrangement. It was first published between 1905 and 1907, with a second, much more extensive, edition appearing between 1927 and 1933. Today all editions and translations of the scheme are controlled by the Universal Decimal Classification Consortium (*http://www.udcc.org*). Several versions of the scheme are available: pocket edition, standard edition, expanded edition. Libraries with large collections should purchase a licence to use the annually updated electronic version of the scheme, the Master Reference File. For many purposes, depending on the subject content of the collection, the pocket edition of the scheme may provide adequate coverage. The pocket edition is very reasonably priced and is used here to devise the examples.

Coverage

UDC's main classes are almost the same as Dewey's:

DDC		UDC	
000	Generalities	0	Generalities
100	Philosophy, psychology	1	Philosophy, psychology

DDC		UDC	
200	Religion	2	Religion
300	Social sciences	3	Social sciences
400	Language	4	(currently vacant)
500	Maths and natural sciences	5	Maths and natural sciences
600	Applied sciences	6	Applied sciences
700	Arts	7	Arts
800	Literature	8	Language, literature
900	Geography, history	9	Geography, history

There are, however, important differences between the two schemes. UDC allows for much more detailed classification than Dewey. DDC, while perfectly adequate for general collections, may lack depth of coverage for specialist topics. UDC incorporates many features of faceted classification, with extensive use of synthesis to create notations for compound subjects. It is this that makes UDC suitable for specialist collections.

UDC includes two types of synthetic device:

- symbols to link notations to allow for the construction of compound numbers for interrelated subjects;
- tables of common and special isolates.

In UDC various facet indicators are used to signify relationships between concepts. These synthetic devices will be explained in more detail below.

Like DDC and LCC, UDC covers all of knowledge and its standard edition provides a detailed listing of subjects.

Universal Decimal Classification: outline

0   Generalities. Science and knowledge. Organisation. Information. Documentation. Librarianship. Institutions. Publications

00   Prolegomena. Fundamentals of knowledge and culture

01   Bibliography and bibliographies. Catalogues

02   Librarianship

030 General reference works [encyclopaedias, dictionaries]

050 Serial publications. Periodicals (their function, business and editorial management)

06   Organisations and other types of cooperation [associations]

070 Newspapers. The press [journalism]

08   Polygraphies. Collective works

09   Manuscripts. Rare and remarkable works

1   Philosophy. Psychology

101 Nature and role of philosophy

11   Metaphysics

122/9 Special metaphysics

13   Philosophy of mind and spirit. Metaphysics of spiritual life

14   Philosophical systems and points of view

159.9 Psychology

16   Logic. Epistemology. Theory of knowledge. Methodology of logic

17   Moral philosophy. Ethics. Practical philosophy

2   Religion. Theology

21   Natural theology. Theodicy. De Deo. Rational theology. Religious philosophy

22   The Bible. Holy scripture

23/28 Christianity. The Christian religion

23   Dogmatic theory

24   Practical theology

25   Pastoral theology

26   Christian church in general

27   General history of the Christian church

28   Christian churches, sects, denominations

29   Non-Christian religions

3   Social sciences. Statistics. Politics. Economics. Trade. Law. Government. Military affairs. Welfare. Insurance. Education. Folklore

30   Theories, methodology and methods in social sciences in general. Sociography

31   Demography. Sociology. Statistics

32   Politics

33   Economics. Economic science

34   Law. Jurisprudence

35   Public administration. Government. Military affairs

36   Safeguarding the mental and material necessities of life. Social work. Social aid. Housing. Insurance

37   Education. Teaching. Training. Leisure

39   Ethnology. Ethnography. Customs. Manners. Traditions. Way of life. Folklore

5   **Mathematics and natural sciences**

50   Generalities about the pure sciences

51   Mathematics

52   Astronomy. Astrophysics. Space research. Geodesy

53   Physics

54   Chemistry. Crystallography. Mineralogy

55   Earth sciences. Geology, meteorology, etc.

56   Palaeontology

57   Biological sciences in general

58   Botany

59   Zoology

6   **Applied sciences. Medicine. Technology**

61   Medical sciences

62   Engineering. Technology in general

63   Agriculture and related sciences and techniques. Forestry. Farming. Wildlife exploitation

64   Home economics. Domestic science. Housekeeping

65   Management and organisation of industry, trade and communication

66   Chemical technology. Chemical and related industries

67   Various industries, trades and crafts

68   Industries, crafts and trades for finished or assembled articles

69   Building (construction) trade. Building materials. Building practice and procedure

7   The arts. Recreation. Entertainment. Sport

71   Physical planning. Regional, town and country planning. Landscapes, parks, gardens

72   Architecture

73   Plastic arts

74   Drawing. Design. Applied arts and crafts

75   Painting

76   Graphic arts. Graphics

77   Photography and similar processes

78   Music

79   Recreation. Entertainment. Games. Sport

8   Language. Linguistics. Literature

80   General questions [Philology. Rhetoric]

81   Linguistics and languages

82   Literature

9   Geography. Biography. History

902/8 Archaeology. Prehistory. Cultural remains. Area studies

91   Geography. Exploration

929 Biographical and related studies

93/94 History

930 Science of history. Ancillary sciences

94   General history

For classifiers acquainted with DDC, UDC's coverage and organisation is very familiar. Its strength lies in the flexibility in the way different subject concepts can be combined, allowing for greater depth of classification for compound and interdisciplinary topics. This flexibility gives UDC more extensive and in-depth coverage.

Universal Decimal Classification: tables

As in DDC, UDC's auxiliary tables list concepts that can be applied to all or several subjects.

Table 1*a*   Coordination. Extension

Table 1*b*   Relation

Table 1*c*   Language

Table 1*d*   Form

Table 1*e*   Place

Table 1*f*   Race, ethnic grouping and nationality

Table 1*g*   Time

Table 1*h*   Subject specification by notations from non-UDC sources

Table 1*k*   General characteristics (materials and persons)

Most are self-explanatory and all will be examined in detail in the next section.

Structure and use

UDC is arranged into 10 main classes, 100 subclasses and their divisions.

UDC: the 10 main classes

0	Generalities. Science and knowledge. Organisation. Information. Documentation. Librarianship. Institutions. Publications
1	Philosophy. Psychology
2	Religion. Theology
3	Social sciences. Statistics. Politics. Economics. Trade. Law. Government. Military affairs. Welfare. Insurance. Education. Folklore
4	[Currently vacant]
5	Mathematics and natural sciences
6	Applied sciences. Medicine. Technology

7	The arts. Recreation. Entertainment. Sport
8	Language. Linguistics. Literature
9	Geography. Biography. History

Each main class is divided into 10 subclasses:

7	The arts. Recreation. Entertainment. Sport
71	Physical planning. Regional, town and country planning
72	Architecture
73	Plastic arts
74	Drawing. Design. Applied arts and crafts
75	Painting
76	Graphic arts. Graphics
77	Photography and similar processes
78	Music
79	Recreation. Entertainment. Games. Sport

Each subclass is further subdivided:

79	Recreation. Entertainment. Games. Sport
791	Public entertainments. Spectacles. Displays
792	Theatre. Stagecraft. Dramatic performances
793	Social entertainments and recreations. Art of movement. Dance. Party games
794	Board and table games (of thought, skill and chance)
795	[Vacant]
796	Sport. Games. Physical exercises
797	Water sports. Aerial sports
798	Riding and driving. Horse and other animal sports
799	Fishing. Hunting. Shooting and target sports

Further subdivisions are listed as appropriate:

794.1	Chess
794.2	Minor board games not dependent on chance
794.3	Table games with pieces or counters and an element of chance

794.4 Card games

794.41 Partner card games

794.5 Pattern games or puzzles requiring patience or dexterity

794.8 Minor aiming games. Children's miniature games

794.9 Games of pure chance

In the pocket edition, subdivision rarely extends beyond three digits after the decimal point, except where built numbers (identified by a diamond symbol) are listed. UDC notations are always broken down into groups of three characters; if no other symbol (colon, plus, equals, etc.) appears, then a point is used (French language is =133.1, not =1331).

Notes

Three types of notes can be identified in UDC. Often a symbol is used, rather than a name, to indicate a type of note. The notes in UDC provide clarification and/or instructions for the classifier:

- Notes that describe what is found in a class;
- Notes that describe what is found in other classes;
- Notes that explain use of special auxiliaries.

Each of these will be examined below. Notes in UDC are not as detailed and ubiquitous as in DDC. This is because UDC is much more flexible and not as bound by rules (that must be strictly adhered to) as DDC.

Notes that describe what is found in a class

Scope notes

Two types of scope note can be identified in the schedules of the pocket edition of UDC. One type of note, always italicised, provides definition and clarification. Example:

81   Linguistics and languages

Philology in the sense of linguistics, especially historical

In the pocket edition depth of subdivision is lacking. In order to specify the contents of a class, a second type of scope note is used quite extensively. These notes area introduced by a special symbol: □ (square), and are self-explanatory. Examples:

794.9   Games of pure chance. □ Dice. Roulette. Lotto (bingo)

577.1   Molecular bases of life. Biochemistry and bio-organic chemistry generally. □ Biopolymers. Proteins. Amino acids. Nucleic acids. Carbohydrates. Lipids. Enzymes. Vitamins. Hormones. Biosynthesis

At some classes, both types of scope note are present. Example:

232.9   Life of Christ. □ Passion. Crucifixion. Resurrection

General accounts of the life of Christ, his person, teachings, works, influence

'Class here' notes

Like scope notes, these tell you what topics are included in a class. Examples:

004   Computer science and technology. Computing

Class here information technology (computing and telecommunications)

504   Environmental science. Environmentology

Class here matters concerning the environment and its components as affected by human activities

'Includes' notes

These occur only very occasionally in the pocket edition. Again they provide definition and clarification. Example:

64   Home economics. Domestic science. Housekeeping

Includes the household and household articles from the point of view of their use; also housekeeping operations and domestic work on a commercial scale (e.g. Hotelkeeping)

Notes that describe what is found in other classes
'See' notes

See notes lead the classifier to an alternative location for narrower aspects of a topic, and may also indicate how a concept is represented in other disciplines. They are also used to direct the classifier to concepts in the tables. Examples:

624 Civil and structural engineering in general

For building materials, trades and construction see 69

For architectural design and purpose see 72

050 Serial publications. Periodicals (their function, business and editorial management)

For serials as form of document, see Table 1d (05)

'Class elsewhere' notes

As in DDC these notes always begin with the word 'class' and lead the classifier to a preferred number for related topics, and/or to a comp-rehensive number for interdisciplinary works. Examples:

621 Mechanical engineering in general. Nuclear technology. Electrical engineering. Machinery

Class information about particular kinds of machinery at the number for the subject (e.g. class mining equipment with mining in 622)

533 Mechanics of gases. Aeromechanics. Plasma physics

Class information about both liquids and gases in 532

Related concept notes

These include see also notes but are mainly notes introduced by a special symbol: $\Rightarrow$ (arrow), directing the classifier to related concepts elsewhere in the schedules. Examples:

659.4 Public relations (PR)

$\Rightarrow$ 354.36

Here the classifier is being directed from PR within the management schedules to PR within public administration and government.

Sometimes the classifier is directed to a broader class:

621.4 Heat engines (except steam engines)

$\Rightarrow$ 621.1

621.1 is the notation for heat engines in general, including steam engines.

Notes that explain use of common and special auxiliaries

In UDC common auxiliaries are found in the tables (outlined above and examined in detail below), whereas special auxiliaries are found throughout the schedules and include concepts that apply to some, but not all, subjects. Examples:

821   Literatures of individual languages

The subdivisions of 821 can be derived from =1/=9 (Table 1c Languages) by substituting a point for the equals sign.

The note here is instructing the classifier to specify the literature of a particular language by using a notation from the common auxiliaries of language. So, to specify literature in Russian, the classifier would add to base number 821 the notation for the Russian language from Table 1*c*: =161.1, replacing the equals sign with a point: 821.161.1

Special auxiliaries are always identified by side-lining:

52   Astronomy. Astrophysics. Space research. Geodesy.

|52–1/–8 properties, processes, parts, etc.

These auxiliaries are applicable only at 52/524

The note here tells the classifier that these special auxiliaries only apply to a range of numbers within the astronomy schedules. To classify a work on the satellites of the planet Neptune:

523.481 Neptune

|52–87   Satellites. Companions

Built notation using the special auxiliaries: 523.481–87

Number building

In the pocket edition of UDC the classifier will find some examples of built numbers, identified by a diamond symbol. However, to realise the full potential of UDC, the classifier has to engage in the process of analysis and synthesis in the same way as when using a fully faceted classification scheme. Analysis involves identifying the individual subject components of a work. Synthesis involves combining the individual subject components to create a notation that expresses the full subject content of the work. Notational synthesis is achieved by using the linking signs: + (plus), / (forward slash), : (colon), together with symbols indicating the use of common auxiliaries.

Common auxiliary signs and subdivisions: Tables 1a–k

Linking signs	+, /, :	(Tables 1a and 1b)
Language	= ...	(Table 1c)
Form	(0/09)	(Table 1d)
Place	(1–9)	(Table 1e)
Race, nationality, etc.	(= ...)	(Table 1f)
Time	" ... "	(Table 1g)
Non-UDC codes, etc.	#, A/Z	(Table 1h)
General characteristics	–0 ...	(Table 1k) currently includes:
Materials	–03 ...	
Persons	–05 ...	

The role and use of each of these will be examined in detail below.

Linking signs

UDC's linking signs are the key to its ability to organise specialist collections. They provide the classifier with a powerful tool with which to describe subjects in impressive detail. It is its linking signs that place UDC close to faceted classification schemes on the classification continuum from enumerative to faceted.

Table 1a: coordination and extension

The symbols in Table 1a extend the meaning of a class number and so provide a means to describe works that provide a broad coverage of topics. Using DDC the classifier often has to use the broadest possible inclusive number to describe works that provide a broad treatment of subjects; this may not fully express its coverage. Using UDC the classifier can express the full coverage of a work in the notation.

The coordination symbol + (plus) connects two or more, non-consecutive, UDC numbers to express compound topics. Examples:

Cereals and fruits:	633.1+634.1
Mineralogy and metallurgy:	549+669
Iran and Iraq:	(55+567)

The extension symbol / (forward slash) connects the first and last number of a series of consecutively listed UDC notations to form a number for a range of topics. Examples:

Physics and chemistry:	53/54
Judaism and Islam	296/297
Attention, learning and creativity	159.952/.954
Arctic and Antarctic	(98/99)

As can be seen in the final examples illustrating the use of coordination and extension symbols, they can link concepts listed in the tables as well as those listed in the main schedules.

Table 1*b*: relation

The relation symbol : (colon) is used to narrow rather than broaden the meaning of a class number. Many types of relationships between subject concepts are possible, for example reciprocal or subsumptive. Use of this symbol does not specify the type of relationship – it simply indicates that one exists. If two or more discrete subjects receive equal treatment in a work, then the plus symbol can be used to link them. If an equal relationship cannot be identified, for example if one subject is examined in the context of another, then the colon should be used to link the notations. Examples:

Aptitude testing in staff recruitment: 159.98:658.3

Either concept can take precedence. In a collection with an emphasis on business and management literature, the preferred order may be: 658.3:159.98

Physiotherapy in relation to sport: 615.8:796

Iran – Iraq War: 94(55:567)"1980/8"

Although not covered in the pocket edition, another type of relationship, the subordinate relationship, can be expressed in UDC using the double colon :: . This can be used to indicate that the subject following the double colon is of less importance than the one preceding it. For most purposes the single colon relationship indicator is adequate.

UDC's linking devices give it a huge advantage over DDC in its ability to fully express compound subjects. Using DDC the classifier often has to choose between two or more subjects when deciding where to classify a work, as only one of the concepts can be represented in the class number. In some libraries copies of the same work are assigned different class numbers to accommodate the needs of different users. This is one way to attempt to overcome the problem of DDC's inflexibility, but it is certainly not to be recommended. UDC's greater flexibility through its use of synthetic devices makes it a better option for specialist collections where depth of classification may be required. This is best illustrated by comparing the two schemes.

Cereals and fruits: UDC: 633.1+634.1   DDC: 633.1 (or 634)

In DDC the only notation to accommodate both concepts within agriculture is 630 agriculture and related technologies. This would be an unacceptably broad representation for most collections and so the classifier has to choose between either cereals or fruits.

Mineralogy and metallurgy: UDC: 549+669
DDC: 549 (or 669.9)

In DDC 669.9 is the notation for physical and chemical metallurgy, which, depending on the treatment of the two subjects, may represent a reasonable compromise.

Iran and Iraq: UDC: (55+567) DDC: –095509567

In DDC use of the 09 standard subdivision allows a notation for a specific geographic area to be added to a geographic area notation *when the first area notation is used to specify the area of origin and the second is used to specify the area where the subject is to be found or practised.* So the above notation could only be used if, for example, a work dealt with Iranians living in Iraq.

Physics and chemistry: UDC: 53/54   DDC: 530 (or 540)

Again, using DDC the classifier has to decide whether to place the work within physics or within chemistry.

Judaism and Islam: UDC: 296/297   DDC: 296.397

The above notation is listed in the DDC schedules. An alternative location would be at 297.282: Islam and Judaism.

Attention, learning and creativity: UDC: 159.952/.954
DDC: 153

In this example, the broadest inclusive DDC number, for conscious mental processes and intelligence, is probably adequate.

Arctic and Antarctic: UDC: (98/99)   DDC: 98

The DDC number represents Arctic islands and Antarctica.

Aptitude testing in staff recruitment: UDC: 658.3:159.98
DDC: 658.31125

This assumes a work emphasising managerial aspects of the subject. The two class numbers could be cited in reverse order using UDC to emphasise psychological testing. The above DDC notation is listed in the schedules. At the number within psychology for aptitude tests, 153.94, is an instruction to add any number from the schedules to specify a field. So, for example, if it suited local needs to classify a work on aptitude testing for secretarial staff within psychology rather than management, then DDC allows for that: 153.94651374.

Physiotherapy in relation to sport: UDC: 615.8:796
DDC: 615.82

This is the DDC number for physiotherapy in general. There is a separate number for sports medicine, 617.1027, but instructions there tell the classifier to class a specific branch of sports medicine with the branch – which, in this instance, is physiotherapy.

Iran–Iraq War: 94(55:567)"1980/8" DDC: 955.0542

In DDC the preferred number (above) locates the conflict within Iranian history. An option allows the classifier to locate it within Iraqi history at 956.70441.

It is clear from the above examples, that where DDC does not specifically list compound topics or include instructions on how to build notations, the classifier has to choose which single topic the work is to be classified and shelved under. Sometimes these choices are easy: one topic receives more in-depth treatment, or the likely readers of the work would expect it to be in a particular part of the library collection. Sometimes these choices are difficult and may involve classification at a broader number than the work merits for example. Using UDC the full subject coverage can be expressed, although the classifier may still have to decide which of the subject components will be cited first and therefore determine shelf location.

Tables of common auxiliaries

Table 1c: language

The common auxiliaries of language in Table 1c are never used alone but can be used after a subject notation to specify the language or linguistic form of a work where necessary. Language auxiliaries are always preceded by an equals sign =.

= ...'0   Origins and periods of language. Phases of development

=00/=03   General concepts

=1/=2   Indo-European languages

=3   Caucasian and other languages. Basque

=4   Afro-Asiatic, Nilo-Saharan, Congo-Kordofanian, Khoisan

=5   Ural-Altaic, Japanese, Korean, Ainu, Palaeo-Siberian, Eskimo-Aleut, Dravidian, Sino-Tibetan

=6   Austro-Asiatic, Austronesian

=7   Indo-Pacific, Australian

=8   American Indian (Amerindian) languages

=9   Artificial languages

Examples:

The Bible in French:	22=133.1
base number for The Bible:	22
add Table 1c notation for French:	=133.1
Poetic works of Heine in German:	821.112.2–1HEINE
base number for literature by language:	821
add modified Table 1c notation for German: .112.2	
(a point replaces the equals sign)	
add special auxiliary for poetry:	–1
add author's name (or abbreviation)	HEINE

Table 1d: form

The common auxiliaries of form in Table 1d are usually preceded by a subject notation, but can be cited first if a decision has been made to shelve works of the same form together. Form auxiliaries are always enclosed in round brackets and begin with a zero.

(0.0...) Physical features, etc.

(01) Bibliographies

(02) Books in general

(03) Reference works

(04) Non-serial separates. Separata

(05) Serial publications. Periodicals

(06) Publications of societies, organisations

(07) Documents for instruction, teaching, study, training

(08) Collected, polygraphic works. Forms. Lists. Illustrations. Business publications

(09) Historical form. Legal and historical sources

Examples:

Dictionary of science:	5(038)
base number for science:	5
add Table 1*d* notation for dictionary:	(038)
Life of Plants (video recording):	(086.8)581
Table 1 notation for video recordings:	(086.8)
add number for botany:	581

This assumes that all video recordings are grouped together. Citation order could be reversed to shelve video recordings with their subject: 581(086.8)

Table 1e: place

The common auxiliaries of place in Table 1*e* are usually preceded by a subject notation, but can be cited first if a decision has been made to create a shelf arrangement based on place. Place auxiliaries are always enclosed in round brackets and begin with the numbers 1–9.

(1) Place and space in general. Localisation. Orientation

(2) Physiographic designation

(3) Places of the ancient world

(4/9) Countries and places of the modern world

(4) Europe

(5) Asia

(6) Africa

(7/8) America, North and South. The Americas

(7) North and Central America

(8) South America

(9) States and regions of the south Pacific and Australia. Arctic. Antarctic.

Examples:

Universities in the developing world:	378(1–773)
base number for universities:	378
add Table 1e notation for developing world:	(1–773)
Family law in the United States:	(73)347.6
Table 1e notation for United States:	(73)
add number for family law:	347.6

This assumes that a law library, for example, would have a primary arrangement under country.

Table 1f: race, nationality, etc.

The common auxiliaries of race, ethnic grouping and nationality in Table 1f are usually preceded by a subject notation, but can be cited first if a decision has been made to create a shelf arrangement based on ethnic groupings or nationalities. Race, nationality, etc. auxiliaries are always enclosed in round brackets and preceded by an equals sign. Particularly effective use is made of systematic mnemonics here, with notations being derived from Tables 1e and 1c.

(=081/=088) degree of development, etc.

(=1–5/–86) various racial affinities

(=1.2/.9) peoples of particular areas and countries
            (*parallel with Table 1e*)

(=11/=8) various races, peoples, linguistic-cultural groups
            (*parallel with Table 1c*)

Examples:

Social psychology of the Chinese people:	316.6(=1.510)
base number for social psychology:	316.6
add Table 1*f* notation for Chinese (from Table 1*e*):	(=1.510)
Inuit death customs:	393(=562)
base number for death customs:	393
add Table 1*f* notation for Inuit (from Table 1*c*):	(=562)

Table 1g: time

The common auxiliaries of time in Table 1*g* are usually preceded by a subject notation, but can be cited first if a decision has been made to create a shelf arrangement based on date. Time auxiliaries are always enclosed in quotation marks. As well as provision for dates, times and eras, abstract concepts are listed, for example permanence. Particularly effective use is made of literal mnemonics in this table, and it is possible to be highly specific (see Iran–Iraq war example above).

"0/2" Dates and ranges of time (AD) in conventional Christian (Gregorian) reckoning

"3" Conventional time divisions and subdivisions: numbered, named, etc.

"4" Duration. Time-span. Period etc. ages and age-groups. Quinquenniums, decades, centuries, millennia, etc.

"5" Periodicity. Frequency. Recurrence at specified intervals. Weekly, monthly, annual, etc.

"6" Geological, archaeological and cultural time divisions. Eras. Geological periods. Ages (ice ages, Stone Age, etc.)

"7" Phenomena in time. Phenomenology of time. Simultaneity, non-simultaneity. Sequence. Permanence, temporariness, etc.

Examples:

Geology of the Mesozoic:	55"615"
base number for geology:	55
add Table 1*g* notation for Mesozoic:	"615"

Sharpeville Massacre:	94(680)"1960"
base number for history:	94
add Table 1e notation for South Africa:	(680)
add Table 1g notation for 1960:	"1960"

Table 1h: non-UDC codes, etc.

Notes in Table 1h give guidance on use of subject specification by notations from non-UDC sources. Such notations should be separated from the UDC number by use of a letter or other symbol – the # (hash) is given as an example in the pocket edition. It is suggested that the source of the code used should be acknowledged. This is particularly useful for chemical compounds, for example. Guidance is also given on the use of proper names, abbreviations and acronyms. These can be added to any UDC number.
Examples:

Halley's Comet:	523.6#81P
base number for comets:	523.6
add period comet number (Minor Planet Center):	#81P
University of Durham:	378.4(410)Durham
base number for universities:	378.4
add Table 1e notation for Britain:	(410)
add name:	Durham

Table 1k: general characteristics

The common auxiliaries of general characteristics in Table 1k must be preceded by a class number from the main schedules. There are currently two listings within this table: materials and persons.

1. The common auxiliaries of materials are always preceded by –03.

–032 Naturally occurring mineral materials

–033 Manufactured mineral-based materials

–034 Metals

–035 Materials of mainly organic origin

–036 Macromolecular materials. Rubbers and plastics

–037 Textiles. Fibres. Yarns. Fabrics. Cloth

–038 Other materials

Examples:

Cane furniture manufacturing:	684.4–035.2
base number for furniture manufacturing:	684.4
add Table 1*k* notation for cane:	–035.2
Amber jewellery:	671.1–032.38
base number for jewellery (crafts):	671.1
add Table 1*k* notation for amber:	–032.38

2. The common auxiliaries of persons are always preceded by –05.

–051 Persons as agents, doers, practitioners (studying, making, serving, etc.)

–052 Persons as targets, clients, users (studied, served, etc.)

–053 Persons according to age or age-groups

–054 Persons according to ethnic characteristics, nationality, citizenship, etc.

–055 Persons according to sex and kinship

–056 Persons according to constitution, health, disposition, hereditary or other traits

–057 Persons according to occupation, work, livelihood, education

–058 Persons according to social class, civil status

Examples:

Public library users:	027.5–052
base number for public libraries:	027.5
add Table 1*k* notation for persons as users, etc.:	–052
NHS care of the elderly:	614.39(410)–053.9
base number for national health services:	614.39
add Table 1*e* notation for Britain:	(410)
add Table 1*k* notation for elderly persons:	–053.9

Citation order and filing order

The concepts of citation order and filing order were examined in Chapter 1. In DDC and LCC, which are enumerative classification schemes, citation order is largely determined in the listing of subjects or in the rules for adding concepts from tables. UDC, with its more faceted approach to classification, allows for much greater flexibility in how concepts are combined in creating a class number. Citation order and filing order of notational elements must, therefore, be considered here.

Filing order

The rule for filing order in UDC is very simple to remember, but appears quite complicated in practice. In general, filing order follows the order of the tables and main schedules, with a progression from the general to the specific. Filing order of UDC, which determines shelf arrangement of materials, is as follows:

Common auxiliaries used independently or to begin a notation:

Language:	=	=131.1	Italian
Form:	(0...)	(086.8)	video recording
Place:	(1–9)	(450)	Italy
Race, etc.:	(=...)	(=1.375)	Etruscans
Time:	"... "	"199"	1990s

Filing order of the above common auxiliaries, all of which may be used independently or at the start of a notation, follows the order of Tables 1*c* to 1*g*.

Next are filed notations using the coordination and extension symbols:

Coordination:	+	634.3+634.8	orange groves and vineyards
Extension:	/	632.3/632.4	bacterial and fungal diseases of plants

Next are filed simple numbers. This may seem counter-intuitive to classifiers familiar with DDC in which briefer notations indicate more general subjects, but in UDC use of coordination and extension broaden the meaning of the class number:

Simple number	634.8	vineyards

Next are filed numbers using the relationship symbol, which narrows the meaning of the class number:

Relation: : 634.8:658.8 marketing and sales in relation to vineyards

Now follow the common auxiliaries in the same order as they appear in Tables 1*c* to 1*k*:

Language:	=	634.8=131.1	item about vineyards in Italian
Form:	(0...)	634.8(086.8)	video recording about vineyards
Place:	(1–9)	634.8(450)	vineyards in Italy
Race, etc.:	(=...)	634.8(=1.375)	vineyards and the Etruscans
Time:	"..."	634.8"199"	vineyards in the 1990s
Non-UDC notation:		634.8C40	vineyards and temperature of 40 degrees Celsius
A–Z specification:		634.8Colorino	vineyards with Colorino grapes
Materials/persons:	–0	634.8–057.117	vineyards and casual workers
Special auxiliaries:		634.8–759	vineyards and security devices

The above filing order should be adhered to at all times. This may not appear to establish a particularly helpful order of subjects for browsing, but it adheres to the principle of broadest subjects first as explored in Chapter 1 and in practice it works rather well because of UDC's flexible *citation* order. For example, if all of the above dealt with Italian vineyards, and a country-by-country treatment was required for items about vineyards, then the place element could, and in the case of language and form, would be cited before the other common auxiliaries in the class number:

Item about vineyards in Italy in Italian: 634.8(450)=131.1

Video recording about vineyards in Italy: 634.8(450)(086.8)

Citation order determines *filing* order.

Citation order

As already mentioned, UDC allows for a degree of flexibility in the order in which notational elements are cited. As good practice dictates, there is a preferred citation order, but this can be modified to accommodate the needs of individual libraries. As discussed in Chapter 1, having determined a citation order, it is important to apply it consistently.

Preferred citation order in UDC moves from the specific to the general: main number, special auxiliaries, common auxiliaries.

First cite main number as follows:

> Cite numbers in ascending order when using linking signs + (addition) and : (relation):
>
> 634.3+634.8 not 634.8+634.3
>
> 634.8:658.8 not 658.8:634.8

Obviously, when using the consecutive extension symbol /, numbers would be cited in ascending order.

Next add any special auxiliaries:

> 634.3+634.8–759

Next add common auxiliaries in the reverse of the filing order:

Persons	–05
Materials	–03
A–Z specification	
Non-UDC notation	
Time	"…"
Race, etc.	(=…)
Place	(1/9)
Form	(0…)
Language	=

Examples:

- Video recording in Italian about the use of casual workers in vineyards in Italy in the 1990s:

Main number, common auxiliaries of persons, time, place, form, language: 634.8–057.117"199"(450)(086.8)=131.1

- Use of security devices in orange groves and vineyards in Italy:

Main number, special auxiliary, common auxiliary of place: 634.3+634.8–759(450)

Preferred citation order moves from the specific subject through increasingly general aspects of a topic in accordance with the general rules for citation order as explained in Chapter 1. However, individual libraries can modify the preferred order to better accommodate local needs. This flexibility is a major strength of UDC.

Notation

The general qualities that notation should possess were introduced in Chapter 1 and have been examined with regard to DDC and LCC in Chapter 2. These qualities will now be examined and evaluated with specific reference to UDC.

Notation must convey order

Main numbers in UDC certainly have a self-evident, numerical order. However, the order in which notational elements are cited and filed is not self-evident and has to be learned. Use of symbols in addition to alphanumeric characters will always have a negative impact in this respect. UDC may seem particularly difficult to the novice user because of the variety of symbols utilised.

The notation should be brief and simple

From the examples given above, it is clear that UDC notations are often lengthy and complex. In fact a UDC class number may be only a single digit in length, so greater brevity than schemes like DDC is possible. So, brevity and simplicity are achievable, but at the expense of depth of classification for composite topics. If depth is to be sacrificed, then the choice of UDC to organise a collection is questionable. The power of UDC lies in its ability to express and differentiate between compound subjects, both interdisciplinary and within disciplines. Use of DDC to organise a specialised library collection may result in the whole collection being shelved at the same number, resulting in what is essentially an author/title arrangement of materials. UDC allows for full and flexible expression of compound subjects, but it cannot achieve this in brief and simple notations.

The notation should be memorable

Systematic mnemonics is the main type of memory aid used in UDC, and this device is used with consistency and to very good effect. DDC's inconsistent use of systematic mnemonics has been noted, for example in the number of zeros used to introduce standard subdivisions. No such inconsistency is present in UDC. In UDC (450) *always* represents Italy (038) *always* represents a dictionary, =111 *always* represents the English language.

Good use is also made of literal mnemonics in UDC. The common auxiliary of time allows dates to be expressed in a literal and instantly recognisable way. For example, the twentieth century is expressed as "19", the 1960s are expressed as "196"; 1966 is expressed as "1966"; 15 February 1966 is expressed as "1966.02.15". Literal mnemonics can also be used in the non-UDC codes and in the A/Z specification which specifically allow for use of standard codes, abbreviations and proper names.

The notation should be hospitable to the insertion of new subjects

As already explored in relation to DDC and LCC, as well as being able to accommodate new subjects, it is important that new subjects are accommodated in their correct place within the classification scheme. There are three ways in which UDC achieves hospitality:

1. *Decimal notation.* As discussed in the context of DDC, UDC allows for a new subject to be fitted almost anywhere in its sequence by using decimal subdivision.

2. *Unassigned notation.* As in DDC and LCC, there are gaps in UDC's listing of subjects into which new topics can be fitted.

3. *Faceted structure.* Often new subjects can be accommodated by linking previously unrelated topics. When interdisciplinary fields of study emerge, notations can be built using the existing schedules. This is a major advantage of using a faceted scheme for specialist collections –

classifiers do not necessarily have to wait until revisions to the scheme are published to classify materials in emerging areas of knowledge.

Notation might show hierarchy: expressiveness

This is a quality one would expect to find in an enumerative classification scheme; it is not a quality usually associated with faceted classification schemes. Nevertheless, in some respects, UDC is more expressive than DDC. As noted above, UDC's minimum length of a notation is one character (as opposed to DDC's three characters):

5	Mathematics and natural sciences;
53	Physics
539	Physical nature of matter
539.1	Nuclear, atomic, molecular physics
539.12	Elementary and simple particles
539.122	Photons

This is highly expressive, moving clearly from the general to the specific. Expressiveness is lost when linking symbols are used to join class numbers and to add common auxiliaries. As noted previously, longer numbers may denote broader rather than narrower topics; for example: 53/54 is broader than 53.

The notation should allow for flexibility

UDC performs extremely well in this respect. The preferred citation order can be modified in a highly flexible way to accommodate the needs of individual libraries. Examples:

■ Law of inheritance in relation to daughters in England in the 19th century:

Preferred citation order:

347.6–055.62–055.2"18"(410.1)

Other possible orders include:

(410.1)347.6–055.62–055.2"18"   *(file under place)*

"18"347.6–0.55.62–055.2(410.1)   *(file under date)*

- Animal behaviour, conference proceedings, 2003, in Russian:
  Preferred citation order:

  591.5"2003"(063)=161.1

  Other possible orders include:

  "2003"591.5(063)=161.1 (*file under date*)

  (063)591.5"2003"=161.1 (*file under form*)

  =161.1:591.5"2003"(063) (*file under language*)

This flexibility allows UDC to be easily adapted to meet local needs, again making it highly suitable to organise specialist collections of materials, where aspects of date or of place, for example, may be of importance in establishing shelf order.

Overview

UDC's coverage in certain areas like religion can be criticised in exactly the same way as DDC's because of their similarities. The complexity of UDC's notations may not make it an ideal choice for large, general library collections: users may find notations difficult to remember and the time needed for shelving and shelf tidying would be increased.

However, it is not suggested that UDC be used in general libraries, but rather to organise specialist collections. Here UDC has many advantages over the general schemes examined in Chapter 2. The depth of classification possible, even using the pocket edition, is very impressive and its flexible citation order allows it to be easily adapted to meet local needs. It is a scheme used throughout the world, is quite well supported by documentation and benefits from regular revisions. Any classifier familiar with DDC should find it relatively easy to adapt to UDC and would welcome its flexibility. In many ways, UDC is easier to use than DDC: rules for building notations are applied consistently and the classifier does not have to check the schedules for special instructions when combining class numbers or adding concepts from tables.

Reference and recommended reading

Foskett, A.C. (1996) Chapter 18 in *The Subject Approach to Information*, 5th edn. London: Library Association.

McIlwaine, I.C. (2000) *The Universal Decimal Classification: A Guide to Its Use*. The Hague: UDC Consortium.

McIlwaine provides good detailed coverage of the use of UDC. Foskett includes a useful overview of its structure and use. A lot of the literature about UDC is rather dated, but a full bibliography and information about the scheme itself and about the published versions of the schedules is available on the web at: *http://www.udcc.org*.

Practical exercises

Using UDC pocket edition, what subjects do the following notations represent?

621.39

639.3

785.7

025.5:027.4

004.08:655.4

53/54 (035)

94(73)"1773"

305–055.2

241–055.52–055.2

551.4(261.6)

821.111–2"15/16"

372.8:511

578.7:614.4

398.2:599.742.1

811.11'282

599.322:591.5

(038)=134.2

395(=521)

Using UDC pocket edition, classify the following:

Human physiology

Animal behaviour

Visual perception

Encyclopaedia of medicine

Neurophysiology

Book of Common Prayer

German grammar

How to play bridge

Education of gifted children

Winter cookery

Research methods in organic chemistry

The Koran (English translation)

Word for Windows manual

History of the trade union movement

Ethics of human cloning

The Prelude by William Wordsworth (*Wordsworth was an English Romantic poet*)

Information retrieval systems in pharmacology

Richard Feynman: a biography (*Feynman was a physicist*)

Drug treatment of Parkinson's disease

Howard Hodgkin: paintings (*Hodgkin is an English artist*)

Nurse education in the United States

Statistical methods in psychology

Fashion in Restoration England

Films of Orson Welles (*Welles as a film director*)

Faceted classification schemes

UDC can be described as a hybrid scheme: it possesses features of both enumerative and faceted classification. In this section, we examine fully faceted classification schemes. Faceted classification, which was developed in the mid-twentieth century, has a shorter history than enumerative classification. Faceted classification relies on synthesis, the fitting together of notational components to specify a subject: the subject components that are fitted together are usually called facets – hence faceted classification schemes. Faceted classification schemes are termed synthetic classification schemes, in technical terminology analytico-synthetic. The technical name reflects the two major activities involved in applying faceted classification: analysis of a subject into facets and synthesis of the facets to create a notation (Hunter, 2002).

The development of synthetic or faceted classification is usually accredited to S.R. Ranganathan who published the first edition of his Colon Classification (CC) in 1933. Certain fundamental aims underlie Ranganathan's Colon Classification as explained in his *Prolegomena to Library Classification* (Ranganathan, 1937). His main aim was to provide a unique language and theory for classification. His objectives were to achieve a helpful filing order, to express fully in a notation the specific subject of each work, and to give the classifier the opportunity to cope with new subjects. Ranganathan developed ideas which could be seen to be evolving in DDC, with its separate listings of recurring concepts in the tables. This idea was developed further in UDC, and Ranganathan, inspired by the writings of Henry Bliss, developed it still further, by devising a fully faceted classification scheme. As well as being respons-ible for CC, Ranganathan is recognised as probably the greatest theorist on classification and has been very influential in the subsequent development of faceted classification schemes for specialist materials and collections.

Faceted classification schemes have not been widely adopted by general libraries in the West. There are two reasons for this:

- DDC and LCC, the most widely used schemes, are perfectly adequate for general library collections. They have comprehensive coverage, are relatively easy to use and provide a helpful order of materials on the library shelves.
- No large library would want to undertake the enormous task of reclassifying its stock. Faceted classification emerged after libraries had already adopted DDC and LCC to organise their materials.

CC was adopted by libraries in Ranganathan's native India, although the trend there now seems to be towards adopting the major enumerative schemes like DDC. This is not surprising given that the latest edition of CC, CC7, was published in 1987 and contains many errors (Foskett, 1996). Any major library needs an up-to-date classification that is error-free and supported by detailed documentation.

Structure and use

Ranganathan's theory of faceted classification is based on the argument that, instead of trying to list all subjects in detail, a classification should first identify main classes or disciplines, in just the same way as enumerative schemes. Then within each main class or discipline, it need only enumerate or list basic concepts. Most subjects are compounds, meaning that they are made up of two or more facets. These facets or elements of a subject can be either specific to that subject or common to all subjects. Facets common to all subjects have already been explored in the sections on DDC and UDC; they include place, time, and form of presentation. Other concepts that can be applied to many but not all subjects are materials, for example steel, and action or process, for example design.

In using a faceted scheme a classifier would analyse the subject of a work into its various facets and then apply notational synthesis. Notational synthesis involves linking together, in a specified order and manner, the symbols representing the subject of the work within these facets to create the notation. Example:

Design of submarines in the United States in the 20th century

Using an enumerative scheme the classifier would probably start by checking the index. In DDC there are several index entries under 'submarines', including 'design' at 623.81257. The next step would be to go to the appropriate place in the schedules and see if instructions are provided about how to add the concepts of United States and 20th century to the notation listed. At 623.8121–.8129 the classifier is instructed how to specify design of a specific type of craft (add numbers following 623.82, which is how the number listed in the index was built) but it is not specified how standard subdivisions of place and time are added to the base number. We therefore assume that they must be preceded by a single zero. Place (0973) and time (0904) can now be added to the base number: 623.8125709730904.

Using a faceted scheme, the classifier would first analyse the subject into its separate components: central concept (submarine), process (design), place (United States), time (20th century). Next the index and schedules of the scheme would be consulted to discover the notation for each of these concepts. These notational elements would then be combined to form the complete notation. In Colon Classification 6th edition (CC6):

> D5254   Submarine (D is main class engineering, 5254 represents submarine)

4   Design in class D (engineering)

73   United States

N   20th century

The complete notation, including the linking symbols, is:

D5254:4.73'N

Use of symbols to link facets in CC will be examined below.

A fully faceted classification scheme does not list subjects in detail like an enumerative scheme; rather it provides a kit from which a notation for any subject can be assembled. Ranganathan (1960) used a Meccano set as an analogy; a more familiar analogy today would perhaps be Lego. Individual pieces can be fitted together to form sophisticated structures.

The advantages cited by supporters of the fully faceted approach to classification are that it is the best way to provide detail and accuracy and that it enables the scheme to keep pace with new developments in knowledge. Enumerative schemes have a built-in obsolescence: they enumerate the state of knowledge at the time they were published and have to be frequently revised to accommodate new subjects. Faceted schemes can often accommodate new subjects by combining notations for existing concepts. Of course, new subjects do have to be added to the schedules of faceted schemes, but this should require less extensive revision than is the case with enumerative schemes. Faceted schemes do not have the rigid structure of enumerative schemes and completely new subjects can be accommodated by simply extending the schedules.

Helpful order of subjects in faceted schemes is achieved by the order of the main classes and subclasses and the order in which facets are combined. In CC, Ranganathan lays down rules for citation order but builds in flexibility by stating that classifiers can to some degree construct their own helpful order which best meets the needs of their particular collection. The basic rule in the case of CC is that which we have already explored in the context of citation order elsewhere: facets are cited so that the most concrete or important facet comes first and the remaining facets are cited in diminishing order of importance. The facet that is cited first will, of course, determine where a book is shelved. Ranganathan devised the citation order: personality, matter, energy, space, time (PMEST). Personality is difficult to define precisely, but can be described as the central concept. In the example above, 'submarine' occupies the personality facet.

The notation in a faceted scheme might need to indicate each change of facet, generally through using some form of punctuation to link each facet, as in UDC's use of different punctuation to identify concepts from the tables. This serves two purposes: it shows where one facet ends and another begins, and it also helps to break up the notation so that it is easier to remember.

To further illustrate these features, two faceted classification schemes devised for use in general collections will be examined in somewhat greater detail.

Colon Classification

Some people find CC difficult to grasp. This may be due, at least in part, to the style of writing used in descriptions and analyses of the scheme, and the fact that Ranganathan himself uses a lot of technical terminology. However, in essence, CC (excluding CC7) is elegantly constructed and quite simple to grasp – in many ways easier to grasp and to use than DDC. In any event, the purpose of this section is not to promote expert use of CC but to further illustrate the concept of faceted classification. Some understanding and study of CC is valuable training in analysing a subject and deciding the sequence in which its constituent elements should be cited in a classmark.

CC6 will be used here to devise examples of its use. It is published in one small volume containing lists of common isolates, main classes and their subdivisions, and an index. CC uses a mixed notation: Roman letters, Greek letters and Arabic numbers. Citation order is controlled by the facet formula PMEST. In CC6 each facet is introduced by a distinctive punctuation mark:

Personality	,	(Comma)
Matter	;	(Semi-colon)
Energy	:	(Colon)
Space	.	(Point)
Time	'	(Apostrophe or point)

Classifiers familiar with CC can recognise the type of facet making up the notation. That is very important because the same symbol (particularly the same number) can mean different things in different facets. For example, :4 signifies design in the energy facet in engineering, but the number 4 denotes a different concept in the place facet where .4 signifies Asia (with the point introducing the place facet and the 4 representing Asia). In CC7 more symbols have been introduced to signify different types of relationships within facets, making it unnecessarily complicated. As mentioned earlier CC7 contains many errors and it has increased in complexity to a degree that makes it very difficult to use. According to Foskett (1996: 323) it does not reflect Ranganathan's contribution to classification theory.

It is very rare that all five facets would be used in classifying a work. However, very often two or more levels of the personality facet are needed, for example: design of submarine diesel engines in the United States in the 20th century. Diesel engine and submarine are both foci in the personality facet, introduced by a comma:

D5254,6466:4.73'N

To construct this notation the classifier would look up concepts in the index. The index indicates which main classes concepts occur in, and also often indicates which facet applies to the concept.

Under 'submarine' in the index is the entry:

D [P]. 5254

D is the main class (engineering)

[P] is the personality facet

5254 is submarine

Under 'diesel engine' in the index is the entry:

D [P]. 6466

In the main class D (engineering), diesel engine belongs in the personality facet.

Under 'design' is the entry:

D [E]. 4. N4. Z [P2], 2673

In the main class D (engineering), design belongs in the energy facet [E] and is represented by the number 4. Design also belongs in the energy facet in main class N (fine arts) and is again represented by the number 4. In main class Z (law), design belongs in the P2 facet (second level personality facet) and is represented by 2673.

Under 'United States' in the geographical division index is: 73

Under '20th century' in the time isolate index is: N 1900–99 AD

Now the classifier combines these elements using the PMEST formula and making use of appropriate punctuation to introduce the various facets. Either 'submarine' or 'diesel engine' could be used to begin the notation, depending on the emphasis of the work and the needs of the collection.

Bliss Bibliographic Classification

Another faceted scheme for use in general library collections that will be briefly described here is the Bibliographic Classification of Henry Bliss (BC). The full schedules for the first edition of BC appeared between 1940 and 1953, with the second edition starting to appear from 1976. Development of the scheme is today continued by the Bliss Classification Association (*http://www.sid.cam.ac.uk/bca/bcahome.htm*).

Bliss believed that the order of the main classes was the most important feature of a classification scheme. In BC all the main classes can be grouped into four main areas: philosophy, science, history, and technologies and arts. Within main classes facets are carefully identified and listed; in places the detail exceeds that found in enumerative schemes. To achieve the most helpful listing of subjects Bliss provided alternative locations for some subjects. For example, economic history can be located in either general history or in economics – the classifier decides which location would best suit their library's needs. Bliss also insisted on brief notation, but classmarks for complex subjects can be very lengthy.

Two characteristics of BC are worthy of mention. First, Bliss believed that an effective classification scheme should reflect the educational and scientific consensus – it should be based on the way in which specialists expect their knowledge to be organised. This is a very important point, and one that will be explored further in the next chapter in the context of taxonomy creation. Second, Bliss stressed the importance of collocation and subordination. Collocation means the bringing together of subjects which have a strong relationship to each other. Subordination means rather more than simply listing subjects from the general to the specific in this context. Bliss used subordination in the sense of *gradation by speciality*. This means that although a number of topics may be equally important, some can be seen as more specialised in that they draw on the findings of others (Mills and Broughton, 1977). Subjects that are dependent in this way should follow the subjects on which they depend. The listing of the main classes in BC has been much admired, although subordination breaks down in the social sciences. For example, physics is based on mathematics and therefore must follow it in the list of main classes. Likewise, we use an understanding of physics in chemistry while astronomy depends upon ideas generated in both physics and chemistry. It has merit as a theory, but is very difficult to sustain in a linear expression of disciplines or subjects.

BC may be familiar as it is used to organise the collections at the University of London's Senate House Library.

Examples:

Human anatomy and physiology:	HD
Visual perception:	ICL
Richard Feynman, biography:	B4 FEY

The above examples demonstrate how BC can achieve brevity of notation.

Special faceted classification schemes

Coverage so far has concentrated on classification schemes that attempt to cover all knowledge. This section explores schemes that take a narrower view, focusing on a specific area of knowledge. Special classification schemes are often created for use in special libraries. Small, specialised library collections tend to have very specialised needs for classification that cannot be met by the major general schemes – all the materials would be classified at the same number or in the same main class. Special classification schemes tend to be based upon faceted principles, so concepts explored in the previous section are of relevance here.

General classifications are often problematic in special libraries because even if they do provide enough detail for specialised literature, the notations are likely to be ridiculously lengthy. Updating of general schemes is also a slow process – new knowledge can take several months to be incorporated (longer in the hard-copy editions), and special libraries are likely to have collections which reflect new knowledge. What is often needed in a special library is a detailed classification for the main subject of interest, and a broader treatment for the rest of knowledge. A special library in the pharmaceutical industry, for example, will need a very detailed classification for materials on drugs and medicine, but there will also have to be provision for materials on subjects like law, ethics, genetics, physiology, botany, etc.

As well as catering for specialist collections, special classification schemes can be developed to reflect the needs of special users, for example in a school library, and to deal with particular physical forms of material such as slides or photographs.

London Classification of Business Studies

An excellent example of a special classification scheme is the London Classification of Business Studies (LCBS), which was developed by and is used at the London Business School. LCBS is faceted and was designed upon analytico-synthetic principles. The scheme consists of 26 main classes and a set of auxiliary schedules.

LCBS main classes

A   Management
AY   Administrative management
AZ   The enterprise
B   Marketing
BZ   Physical distribution management
C   Operations management
D   Research and development
E   Finance and accounting
F   Human resource management
G   Industrial relations
J   Economics
JZ   Transport and transport planning
K   Industries
L   Behavioural sciences
M   Communication
N   Education
P   Law
Q   Political science
R   Philosophy, science and technology
S   Management science
T   Operational research
U   Statistics

V   Mathematics

W   Computers and Information technology

X   O & M and work study

Y   Information science

Auxiliary schedules

1   People and occupational roles

2   Industrial products and services

3/4 Standard subject divisions

5   Geographical divisions

6   Time

7   Form divisions

The letters I and O are not used to signify main classes. This is common practice in schemes using Roman letters in notation because they could be mistaken for the numbers one and zero.

LCBS provides very detailed coverage of its subject area and possesses many of the features desirable in a classification scheme. It achieves a helpful order of subjects, notations are brief and simple, and it is hospitable to the addition of new subjects. Main classes are represented by Roman letters and auxiliaries are represented by Arabic numerals, so they can be easily differentiated. Concepts within main classes are combined simply using a forward slash and a space is used to introduce auxiliaries. This simplicity is very welcome as classifiers and users do not have to learn a system of abstract symbols. One of the major drawbacks of UDC and CC is the complexity of the notations. Any notation in a classification scheme is a code and is a symbolic rather than a literal representation, but perceived complexity decreases as fewer symbols are used. LCBS's preferred citation and filing order is alphabetical, but classifiers can cite elements of the notation in any order. Again, the simplicity and flexibility of the scheme are to be commended.

Examples:

■ Trade unions in the car industry:

    trade unions: GC
    car industry: KHB
                     GC/KHB

- Recruitment in public sector organisations in the UK:

public enterprise:	AZE
recruitment:	FB
UK:	511
	AZE/FB 511

- Use of interviews in market research

market research:	BD
interviews:	4171
	BD 4171

The above examples show how LCBS can be used to create brief and simple notations for quite complex topics.

Creating a faceted classification scheme

Libraries with narrowly focused collections may find that existing classification schemes do not provide adequate subject coverage or a helpful shelf arrangement of materials. This section does not, however, only apply to libraries whose entire collections are highly specialised. Most libraries will not need to classify or reclassify their whole collection, but many may have special collections that are not fully exploited and would benefit from reorganisation. A solution may be to create a new classification scheme to meet local needs. In one sense this is quite a straightforward process. As will be outlined below, creation of a classification scheme can be a relatively quick and simple process. However, practical implementation of a new scheme will be a resource-intensive and costly operation, involving creation of new indexes, recataloguing, relabelling and reshelving or refiling of materials.

If a decision is taken to reclassify, and existing schemes do not seem to provide adequate coverage, then the development of a special classification scheme must start from a very clear perspective of the role it is going to play in the library. A first and very obvious question to ask is why is a new scheme being created, why cannot an existing scheme be used? It is important to remember that lots of classification schemes already exist, many of them not associated with the library environment. If there is a need to organise a collection of music CDs or motion picture videos, then why not adopt the classification used in record and video stores? Usability is the key. The aim should be to improve access to the collection, not to engage in an intellectual exercise. An understanding of the needs of the likely users of the scheme is vitally important – how do they approach information? how is their understanding of the subject best represented? Perhaps the users would prefer a purely alphabetical rather than a logical arrangement of materials.

It is also important to realise that the scope of a scheme which focuses on a relatively narrow area may actually be quite wide once all fringe topics have been catered for. Having determined the need for a new classification scheme the first task is to define core topics and then to consider the range of peripheral topics that have to be included. Certainly a comprehensive listing of subjects is essential. A top-down or bottom-up approach can be used to create the comprehensive topic listing. The top-down method would begin with identifying main classes within which associated concepts would be listed. This may appear to be a natural way to approach the problem, but it is rather proscriptive. It may be better to compile a comprehensive topic list before making decisions about how the subject should be organised – the bottom-up method.

Structure: facets, classes and subclasses

Most subjects can be broken down into discrete elements or facets. Various formulae exist that can help to determine the facets represented in a classification scheme and the order in which they are presented. We have already considered citation order in Chapter 1 and in the context of UDC and CC in this chapter, but it is useful to provide an overview of facet formulae at this point. Examples:

Concrete – Process	(Kaiser, 1911)
Thing – Part – Material – Action – Agent	(Coates, 1960)
Personality – Matter – Energy – Space – Time	(Ranganathan, 1960)
Substance, product, organism – Part, organ, structure – Constituent – Property and measure – Object of action, raw material – Action, operation, process, behaviour – Agent, tool – General property, process, operation – Space – Time	(Vickery, 1960)
Thing – Kind – Part – Material – Property – Process – Operation – Agent – Space – Time	(Standard citation order: McIlwaine, 2000)

Some are clearly more complicated than others, but all move from the specific to the general. Any of the above could be modified to meet the needs of a particular collection or group of users.

Having identified the various facets present in the collection, individual subject concepts can be assigned to each facet. The facets themselves may become the main and auxiliary classes; in any event it will be possible to identify classes and perhaps several levels of subclasses. The listing of subjects must, as already noted, be comprehensive. It is also often possible to anticipate subjects that are not currently represented in the collection but may be in the future. An obvious example would be allowing for future dates in the time facet.

Concepts within classes must be listed in some recognisable order. Possible arrangements include:

- Logical: showing conceptual relationships

  For example: mathematics, physics, chemistry (gradation by speciality)

- Procedural: showing progression

  For example: writing a CV, filling out a job application, interview technique

- Chronological: showing movement through time

  For example: Pre-Cambrian, Cambrian, Ordovician, Silurian

- Alphabetical: where no other relationships can be identified, or where an alphabetical arrangement will be most helpful to users of the collection

Notation

In this section the basic principles of an effective notation will be outlined. These will be illustrated and further explored in the next section which outlines a faceted classification scheme for a hypothetical library collection.

Notation must convey order

As the notation determines shelf-order, it is obviously important that it does so unambiguously. Users of the scheme in the English-speaking world would be most likely to be familiar with Roman letters and Arabic numerals which have a self-evident order. Care must be taken if using a mixed notation: would 12AB come before or after AB12?

The notation should be brief and simple

Brevity of notation can be achieved simply by using letters (with a base of 26) rather than numbers (with a base of 10). Brevity can also be achieved by discarding redundant information. For example, if a collection only contains works about motion pictures, then it is not necessary to represent the concept of 'motion picture' in the notation. Brevity increases simplicity and simplicity can also be achieved by limiting the range of symbols used. For example, each change of facet does not necessarily have to be identified by use of a different symbol if care has been taken to ensure the same character or group of characters is not used to represent different concepts in different facets.

The notation should be memorable

Literal and systematic mnemonics should be used as appropriate. However, because helpful order of subjects is often lost, literal mnemonics should be used sparingly, unless their application can be clearly justified, for example in a children's library. Literal mnemonics can be used to good effect in a time facet as was seen in the section on UDC. Systematic mnemonics should be used where possible as they are a powerful memory aid and do not compromise the structure of the scheme as a whole.

The notation should be hospitable to the insertion of new subjects

As already explored in relation to DDC and LCC, as well as being able to accommodate new subjects, it is important that new subjects are inserted in their correct place within the classification scheme. This can be achieved by leaving gaps in the notation, a device used by enumerative schemes, and by providing guidance on how to extend schedules to accommodate new subjects.

Notation might show hierarchy: expressiveness

This is a quality one would expect to find in an enumerative classification scheme, it is not a quality usually associated with faceted classification schemes.

The notation should allow for flexibility

A preferred citation order should be specified, but it is good practice to allow for flexibility as was seen in UDC and LCBS.

Faceted classification scheme for a photographic library

The purpose of this section is to demonstrate that, having grasped the principles of classification generally and faceted classification in particular, it is a relatively straightforward process to create a classification scheme for a specialist library collection. The scheme presented below is not fully developed, as it has been devised in the space of a few hours for a purely imaginary collection of materials, yet it illustrates how depth of subject coverage can be achieved with a limited range of concepts represented.

The hypothetical collection consists of photographs of London from the 1840s to the present day. Of concern to the users of the collection is the content of the images – it is to be used as a document of social history, not as a record of photographic processes.

Notation

A very important point to note is that devising the notation for a scheme should be the last stage in its creation. Subject concepts should be listed and clustered within classes or facets before an attempt is made to assign a notation. This approach takes much less time and effort that trying to fit subjects into an existing notational structure. Having created the clusters of topics, devising and assigning the notation is a quick and simple process.

Notation must convey order

The notation uses Roman letters and Arabic numerals which have a self-evident order.

The notation should be brief and simple

Brevity is achieved by using letters rather than numbers except in the Time facet. Simplicity is aided by limiting the range of symbols used. Notational elements are separated by a space, when representing more than one concept from the same class, the initial letter is ignored and concepts linked by a forward slash, for example Men and Women: Ka/b.

The notation should be memorable

The Time facet uses literal mnemonics.

The notation should be hospitable to the insertion of new subjects

New subjects can be accommodated by adding to the existing list, for example Ferries: Cp (although alphabetical arrangement is lost) and by extension of notation, for example Cricket: Daa, Football: Dab.

Notation might show hierarchy: expressiveness

Expressiveness was sacrificed to maintain brevity.

The notation should allow for flexibility

Preferred citation order is alphabetical, but any facet can be cited first if a particular theme receives prominent treatment. If a chronological sequence is required, then the individual year or decade can be cited first.

A: Institutions

Aa: Church

Ab: Education

Ac: Finance

Ad: Government

Ae: Health

Af: Home and family

Ag: Law

Ah: Royalty

B: **Industry and commerce**

Ba: Industry

    Bb: Docks

    Bc: Factories

    Bd: Workshops

Bh: Commerce

    Bj: Business

    Bk: Retail (*shops and stores*)

    Bl: Markets

    Bm: Street trade

C: **Transport**

Ca: Private

    Cb: Cars

    Cc: Cycles

    Cd: Motorcycles

Ch: Public

    Cj: Buses

    Ck: Taxis

    Cl: Trains

    Cm: Trams

    Cn: Underground

Cs: Commercial

    Ct: Road (*carts, vans, trucks*)

    Cu: Water (*barges, boats, ships*)

D: **Sports and entertainments**

Da: Sports

Db: Games

Dd: Entertainments and leisure activities

De: Exhibitions and galleries

Df: Fairs and circuses

Dg: Leisure and relaxation

Dh: Parties

Dj: Street entertainment

Dk: Theatre and cinema

H: Events

Ha: Celebration

Hb: Ceremony

Hc: Conflict

Hd: Protest

[Life cycle]

Hj: Birth

Hk: Marriage

Hl: Illness

Hm: Death

[Special occasions]

Hr: Birthday

Hs: Christmas

Ht: Easter

Hu: Feast days

J: Materials and products

Ja: Inorganic and synthetic

Jb: Organic

Jc: Fabrics and textiles

Jf: Goods and products

Jg: Clothing

Jh: Household goods

Jj: Natural produce and foodstuffs

Jl: Bread and cereals

Jm: Fruit and vegetables

Jn: Meat and fish

Jr: Luxury products

K: People

By gender

Ka: Male

Kb: Female

By age

Kc: Children

Kd: Youth

Ke: Adults

Kf: Elderly

By race

Kg: European

Kh: African (*black people*)

Kj: Arabic

Kk: Hebraic

Kl: Indic

Km: Oriental

Kn: Romany

By disability

Ks: Physical disabilities

Kt: Mental disabilities

By status

Ku: Upper-classes

Kv: Middle-classes

Kw: Lower-classes (class here the poor)

Kx: Underclasses

L: Space

La: Buildings

    Lb: Private

    Lc: Public

Ld: Streets and squares

Le: Parks and gardens

Lf: Rivers and bridges

[Areas]

Lj: City

      Ll: East End

      Lm: West End

      Ln: Other areas and suburbs

[Specify name as appropriate: Aa La St. Pauls, Ld Piccadilly]

R: Time

Of day

Ra: Morning

Rb: Afternoon

Rc: Evening

Rd: Night

Of year

Re: Spring

Rf: Summer

Rg: Autumn

Rh: Winter

1–2: Individual years and decades

Abbreviate as appropriate:

1853

185: 1850s

196/7: 1960s and 1970s

Examples:

Barges on the Thames, 1862:	Cu 1862 (can specify further if needed: Lf Thames)
Dockers, 1900s:	Bb Kw 190
Matchgirl 1860s:	Bm Kb/c 186
Car salesman, East End, 1960s:	Bh Cb Ka Ll 196
Funeral of Queen Victoria, 1901:	Ah Hm 1901
Buses on Oxford Street, 1959:	Cj Ld Oxford St 1959

Street party, 1945:	Dh Ld 1945
Sunbathers in Hyde Park, 1976:	Dg Le Rf 1976
Children's street games, 1920s:	Db Kc 192
Billingsgate market, 2001	Bl Jn 2001
Family watching television, 1950s:	Af Dg Lb 195
State opening of Parliament, 1990:	Ad Hb 1990

As can be seen from the examples above, a good level of detail can be achieved in relatively brief and simple notations. The classification scheme is certainly not complete and is by no means perfect or free from errors. If a scheme was being developed for a real collection, then days or weeks rather than hours would be spent in analysing the content of the collection and devising the best possible structure. The above scheme is simply used to demystify the process and to illustrate how a classification scheme for a specialised collection can be created.

Overview

Faceted classification schemes designed for use in general libraries (CC and BC) are unlikely to provide a useful classification for specialised collections: they tend to be rather complicated and are not revised frequently enough to keep pace with new areas of knowledge. A practical alternative for a library wishing to organise a special collection of materials would be to create a new classification scheme based on faceted principles.

Such a scheme can be devised relatively quickly and will be tailor-made to meet the demands of the subject area. Choices can be made to ensure the scheme meets the needs of both the collection and its users. If a scheme is to be devised for a children's collection, notation can be designed to possess brevity, simplicity and literal mnemonic qualities for example. If a scheme is to be designed to meet the needs of expert users, then depth of classification can be emphasised.

References

Coates, E.J. (1960) *Subject Catalogues: Headings and Structure.* London: Library Association.

Foskett, A.C. (1996) *The Subject Approach to Information*, 5th edn. London: Library Association, p. 316.

Hunter, E.J. (2002) *Classification Made Simple*, 2nd edn. Aldershot: Ashgate.

Kaiser, J. (1911) *Systematic Indexing*. London: Pitman.

McIlwaine, I.C. (2000) *The Universal Decimal Classification: A Guide to Its Use*. The Hague: UDC Consortium, p. 39.

Mills, J. and Broughton, V. (1977) *Bliss Bibliographic Classification: Introduction and Auxiliary Schedules*, 2nd edn. London: Butterworths, pp. 50–1.

Ranganathan, S.R. (1937) *Prolegomena to Library Classification*. Madras: Madras Library Association.

Ranganathan, S.R. (1960) *Colon Classification*, 6th edn. Bombay: Asia Publishing House, p. 12.

Vickery, B.C. (1960) *Faceted Classification: A Guide to Construction and Use of Special Schemes*. London: Aslib, p. 30.

Recommended reading

Foskett, A.C. (1996) *The Subject Approach to Information*, 5th edn. London: Library Association.

Hunter, E.J. (2002) *Classification Made Simple*, 2nd edn. Aldershot: Ashgate.

Ranganathan, S.R. (1937) *Prolegomena to Library Classification*. Madras: Madras Library Association.

Vickery, B.C. (1960) *Faceted Classification: A Guide to Construction and Use of Special Schemes*. London: Aslib.

Of the above, only Hunter is an easy read, but anyone wishing to explore the principles of faceted classification in depth is recommended to attempt the other texts cited. It would also be worthwhile to read the introductions to the various schemes covered in this section.

Practical exercises

Using the classification scheme for a photographic library, classify the following:

Brixton riots, 1981

University graduation ceremony, 2004

Regent Street Christmas lights, 1987

Football players on Hackney Marshes, 1930s

Houses of Parliament

Funfair at Battersea Park, 1950s

Petticoat Lane market, 2001

Anti-war rally, Hyde Park, 2003

Street entertainers, Covent Garden, 1994

Big Issue seller, Strand, 2002

4

Classifying electronic resources

This chapter acknowledges that any library has increasing numbers of electronic resources that need to be classified. There is currently much interest in the concept of information architecture which incorporates key elements of library technical processes: cataloguing (metadata), classification (taxonomy) and indexing and thesaurus construction (ontology). The latter two concepts are of relevance here, where principles of library classification and classification schemes examined in previous chapters are extrapolated into the digital information environment with an examination of subject trees, taxonomies and ontologies. This involves exploring a range of concepts that have been largely ignored in previous chapters that have focused on classification schemes rather than on indexing generally.

To fully understand the value of classification in the electronic environment it is necessary to explore concepts of controlled vocabularies and thesaurus construction. Additionally, it is important to consider the types of search behaviour that classification of digital resources encourages, so here we have an examination of browsing strategies in the context of subject trees. In the sections on subject analysis and on faceted classification schemes, the concept of meeting user needs and expectations was introduced. This is also treated in greater depth in this chapter, with an exploration of user-centred issues in taxonomy creation.

Vocabulary control and thesaurus construction

We have already touched upon vocabulary control in the context of alphabetical subject indexes to classification schemes in Chapter 1. Here the concept is explored within the context of thesaurus construction.

The basic principles of thesaurus construction are of relevance in a study of subject trees, taxonomies and ontologies.

Rowley provides a definition of a thesaurus:

> a compilation of words and phrases showing synonyms, hierarchical and other relationships and dependencies, the function of which is to provide a standardized vocabulary for information storage and retrieval systems. (Rowley, 1992)

The primary function of a thesaurus is to show semantic relationships between terms: relationships based on their meaning, i.e. what a classification scheme does, but with terms arranged alphabetically. The thesaurus is also an agent of vocabulary control showing terms which may and may not be used in an index. Thesauri tend to concentrate on specific subject areas, for example the *Thesaurus of Psychological Index Terms*, the *Inspec Thesaurus for Physics, Electronics and Computing*, the *ERIC Thesaurus for Education and Related Fields*, the *Assia Thesaurus for the Social Sciences*, etc.

A thesaurus is an alphabetical listing of preferred index terms (descriptors), and terms which should not be used as index headings but which guide the user to the preferred terms (non-descriptors). Under each descriptor various words or abbreviations are used to clarify meaning or indicate relationships with other terms. The most common are:

SN   scope note. Defines the term.

UF   use for. Indicates the descriptor is the preferred term. For example:

   Businesses   UF   firms

Then under Firms:

   Firms   use   businesses

BT   broader-term. This links the term to another higher up the hierarchy of relationships. For example:

   Drama   BT   arts

NT   narrower-term. This links the term to others lower down the hierarchy of relationships. For example:

   Arts   NT   drama

RT   related term. This links the term to others on the same level of the hierarchy of relationships. For example:

Drama   RT   performing arts

Thesaurus construction

Thesaurus construction bears many similarities to creating a classification scheme. The starting point is to define a subject area, for example the range of subjects covered by a particular library or organisation. The next step is to list all the concepts within that subject area, and all the terms associated with those concepts. Next it is necessary to identify relationships between terms. Two types of relationship are of relevance here: equivalence relationships and associative relationships. Identification of equivalence relationships can be used to eliminate synonyms and provide vocabulary control. If two or more terms are seen to be equivalent, in that they describe the same concept, then only one of those synonymous terms will be used as a descriptor. The other terms will be entry points in the index or thesaurus – linked to the preferred term by 'use' or 'see' references. The second type of relationship is the associative relationship: terms that are conceptually related. Terms that have associative relationships are linked using BT, NT and RT references to specify the nature of the association. Only terms used as descriptors have the full array of associative relationships displayed alongside them.

In the process of identifying relationships, a hierarchical structure will begin to emerge, precisely the kind of structure found in an expressive classification scheme. The ordering of subjects in the schedules of a classification scheme is logical, based on a conceptualisation of how knowledge is organised. For example, in DDC at 617.5: regional medicine, the order of the schedules is:

617.51   head

617.52   face

617.53   neck

617.54   thorax (chest) and respiratory system

617.55   abdominal and pelvic cavities

617.56   back

617.57   upper extremities

617.58   lower extremities

This is literally a top-down approach. In a thesaurus the order would be alphabetical:

abdominal and pelvic cavities

back

face

etc.

For each descriptor in the alphabetical list a series of relationships would be made explicit. For example:

neck

BT   regional medicine

NT   larynx and trachea

        pharynx

        throat

        thyroid and parathyroid glands

RT   face

        head

        thorax and respiratory system

        etc.

Having established the relationships, they can be displayed in a hierarchy or subject tree (see Figure. 4.1).

Figure 4.1　Subject tree

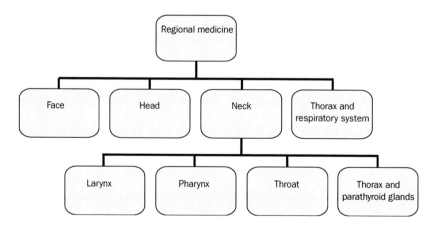

Subject trees

Subject trees will be familiar to anyone using the Web for information searching. Web directories utilise a subject tree structure that provides a browsing environment for searchers. The distinction between web directories and search engines has become very fuzzy, but directories and search engines have very different approaches to information retrieval. The subject trees provided by web directories like the Open Directory (*http://www.dmoz.org*) provide the same information structure as traditional enumerative classification schemes, displaying subjects in a hierarchy and making explicit their relationships to one another. Just as classification schemes like DDC enable library users to browse in the physical library environment, so subject trees enable searchers to browse in the virtual space of the digital information environment.

It is useful at this point to explore the concept of browsing as a search tactic. Enumerative classification schemes with expressive notations organise for browsing, and browsing is a way of searching for information that is very familiar and very much taken for granted by library users. Digital resources can also be organised in such a way as to promote browsing, and again, it is an activity that is widespread but not necessarily fully understood by those practising it. To fully comprehend the rationale for classification of digital information it is important to examine the search behaviour it supports.

In the introductory chapter, classification was described as an innate ability, something we all do on a largely unconscious level in interacting with the world. Likewise we have an innate ability to browse. Browsing for information is so natural to us that we do not recognise the complexity of the behaviour we are engaging in. The concept of browsing is often associated with a rather aimless perusal of materials in a library or bookshop. This ignores its complexity and its value as a means of information retrieval. At least three types of browsing activity can be identified:

- exploratory or serendipitous browsing;
- purposeful browsing, initiated by a need for information on a particular subject;
- focused browsing, often focused on particular sources that we know to be useful.

'Serene dipping' into things as exemplified by Horace Walpole's *Three Princes of Serendip* is the type of behaviour most commonly associated with browsing. Certainly chance discovery of useful information is something everyone has experienced and enjoyed. Often, though, even this type of broadly exploratory browsing originates in a real but perhaps ill-defined need for information. One of the main values of browsing as a way of searching for information is that it allows users to broaden their sphere of interest and expose themselves to information they would not otherwise have encountered. On the other hand, browsing can be very narrowly focused, centring on a particular aspect of a subject or on a few specific sources. Whatever type of browsing activity is being engaged in, this type of exploratory search behaviour is enabled by classification.

Meadow, writing in 1970, describes browsing activities in the library context but he is describing a type of strategy that can be used in searching digital information resources:

> In using a card catalogue or in scanning shelves of books, we commonly employ a complex strategy called browsing. We enter this process with a general idea of the subject of the search or even with a few very specific descriptors – perhaps title or author. If we find just what we want on the basis of the original 'query', the procedure ends. If not, we are likely to begin to search for alternative spellings, variants of subject heading terms, or different classifications under which our subject may have been classified. The routine proceeds so smoothly and informally that we may not recognise its basic nature. (Meadow, 1970)

Meadow is raising several important points here:

- he is describing a systematic search process;
- he suggests that browsing is a comfortable and natural way to search for information;
- he touches on the value of browsing as a means of expanding and extending a search for information.

If, as Meadow suggests, browsing is a valuable and comfortable way to search for information then clearly it must be supported by digital information systems. In the past, so-called browsing interfaces tended to be alphabetical lists of subject headings that presented a rather crude alternative to keyword searching. Today we have much more sophisticated browsing interfaces as exemplified in web directories and Internet or intranet taxonomies.

Web directories

We all know that libraries organise for browsing. Classification schemes provide a subject arrangement of books on shelves and subject groupings help browsers because they can identify which part of the library to browse in. Digital information retrieval systems can also organise for browsing. Web directories provide a browsing environment: menus are used to navigate hierarchies, guiding the user through a series of choices to increasingly specific information. A subject tree provides a structured and organised hierarchy of named categories that can be browsed for information on particular subjects. Under each category or subcategory, links are provided to further categories or web pages. Web pages are assigned to a category by their authors or by subject tree administrators. The best known web directories are Yahoo (*http://www.yahoo.com*) and the Open Directory (*http://www.dmoz.org*), although most major search engines and web portals incorporate a directory to facilitate structured browsing.

The first step in using a web directory to search for information is to decide which top-level category will contain the needed information, just as in deciding which main class in a library classification scheme a topic will be located within. For example, using the Open Directory to search for information on library classification, on the home page the top-level categories offered are shown in Table 4.1.

It is not immediately obvious where the topic of library classification will be located. There is a subcategory, *libraries*, under the top-level category *reference*, and clicking on that link takes the user to a listing of lower-level categories that include *library and information science*. Following that link, the user is taken to a further list of categories, including *technical services*. A further click reveals the category *cataloguing*. Following that link we see the category *classification*, and an indication that 39 records are contained within that subcategory. A final click takes us to a final listing of subcategories including: *Bliss Bibliographic Classification, Colon Classification, Dewey Decimal, Library of Congress, Subject-Specific Schemes, SuDocs* and *UDC*. All these categories contain fewer than ten links to websites, so recall is low, but all sites listed are of high quality. At this level of the hierarchy there is also a list of links to websites, web pages and discussion groups focusing on aspects of library classification. There is also a link to *classification* within the *knowledge management* subcategory that gives us additional links under software.

Table 4.1	Open Directory top-level categories	
Arts Movies, Television, Music…	**Business** Jobs, Real Estate, Investing…	**Computers** Internet, Software, Hardware…
Games Video Games, RPGs, Gambling..	**Health** Fitness, Medicine, Alternative…	**Home** Family, Consumers, Cooking…
Kids and Teens Arts, School Time, Teen Life…	**News** Media, Newspapers, Weather…	**Recreation** Travel, Food, Outdoors, Humor..
Reference Maps, Education, Libraries…	**Regional** US, Canada, UK, Europe…	**Science** Biology, Psychology, Physics
Shopping Autos, Clothing, Gifts…	**Society** People, Religion, Issues…	**Sports** Baseball, Soccer, Basketball…
World Deutsch, Español, Français…		

An overview of the route taken is:

Reference: libraries: library and information science: technical services: cataloguing: classification

Alternative routes would have been:

Society: social sciences: library and information science: technical services: cataloguing: classification

Or:

Science: social sciences: library and information science: technical services: cataloguing: classification

This demonstrates that a more flexible categorisation is possible in the digital environment, with several different routes taking the user to the same information.

If the aim is to find what has been published on the Web on a broad topic, then browsing a subject tree in a web directory like the Open Directory is a very good place to start. A problem is the size of the index. Because web directories rely on humans for their overall design and maintenance, they typically provide links to a smaller number of web pages than the automatically indexed search engines. Conducting a search for classification on Google (*www.google.co.uk*) returned 'about 14,800,000' results. This is impressive recall, but creates problems for the searcher in that a large number of records, many of which do not deal with library classification, have to be browsed and evaluated. The small size of the web directories' indexes is somewhat countered by the greater likelihood of retrieving precisely focused and high-quality information because of the intermediation of the human indexer.

There are four problems associated with web directories and subject trees that have to be considered.

Lack of vocabulary control

Web directories are, in technical terminology, pre-coordinate indexes. This simply means that coordination of terms is performed by an indexer at the time the documents are being indexed. Something that is generally agreed to be essential in pre-coordinate indexes, including book indexes and classification schemes themselves, is vocabulary control. Although the naming and listing of subject categories in web directories like Yahoo and the Open Directory can be said to impose some sort of vocabulary control, the problem is that there is a lack of consistency in use of terms even within the subject tree provided by a single web directory. This lack of consistency in use of terms is even more apparent if different subject trees are compared. For example, the Looksmart directory (*http://search .looksmart.com/*) has 'computing' as a top-level category while most other directories use the word form 'computers'.

Ad hoc addition of new subject categories

Librarians using traditional classification schemes like Dewey often have problems when new subjects emerge because it takes a while for the scheme to be revised to accommodate them. Web indexers do not have that problem: they can simply create a new category and find a place for it in their existing subject tree. This freedom results in some rather bizarre categories at times: in the past the Lycos directory (*http:// www.lycos.com*) has had Pokemon as a top-level category. It can be argued that this is a truly user-centred approach in that the most popular searches are given the status of top-level categories, but the long-term result is that categorisation is constantly changing, and this can be confusing for regular users of the web directory. This approach is most fully exploited in the *An Experiment in Web Indexing* directory (*www.aeiwi.com*) that displays its top 100 searches on its home page.

Limitations of hierarchies

Hierarchies are generally quite effective ways to map subjects, but as we can see looking at any traditional hierarchical classification scheme, hierarchies tend to break down as their size and complexity increases. This was examined in the context of expressiveness of notation and is illustrated by, for example, DDC's engineering schedules.

Limitations of the human indexer

There are three major issues here: the size of the database, the currency of the database and consistency.

Human indexers obviously work more slowly than a software package that automatically indexes web resources. Consequently the databases of web directories are a lot smaller than those of the search engines. The Open Directory is the largest of the web directories and claims to index over four million websites while the Google search engine claims over four billion web pages.

In terms of currency, there may often be a delay in indexing sites or web pages. Also, a user of a web directory may find that they follow the hierarchy to sites or pages that no longer exist. Because human indexers work relatively slowly, keeping the hierarchy current is a huge problem. Information on the Web is often so transient that no retrieval system can claim to be right up to date. Currency is, however, more difficult to maintain in web directories where the links are created by human indexers.

Finally, consistency can be difficult to maintain. In one sense the naming of categories can be argued to increase consistency because searching is not dependent on the presence, or otherwise, of keywords in the text of documents or in the metatags assigned by their authors. However, the teams of people working on indexing the Web for directories like Yahoo cannot invest much time in subject analysis and they can classify items wrongly, which means they end up in the wrong category in the wrong part of the hierarchy. The Open Directory is maintained by volunteers which ensures the quality of the sites indexed but results in rather uneven coverage, depending on the particular subject interests of the indexers.

Unfortunately some of these problems cannot be easily resolved. Hierarchies have limitations – we have to accept that. What would help towards consistency would be standardisation: a formal classification scheme for web resources that would provide a standardised subject tree structure and would also ensure vocabulary control. This is obviously very difficult to implement because of lack of cooperation between the various providers of search facilities. Standardisation was never achieved between the providers of traditional online information retrieval tools like Dialog and Orbit even though their customers were demanding it. The problem is that standardisation of the search interface is very good for the user but it is not very good for the service provider because their customers can switch between service providers too easily. The most respected web directory, and one that perhaps comes closest to promoting standardisation, is the Open Directory. On the other hand, while lack of standardisation may offend the classification theorist, it does allow the web directories to accommodate a whole range of different users and user needs. Users with more formal information needs are accommodated by the Open Directory while other users may prefer the categorisations offered by AOL and MSN.

Various projects are exploring the possibility of replacing the human indexer with software to achieve automatic classification of resources. For example, the OCLC has explored using Dewey Decimal for automatic classification of the Web. But, at the moment, there is no real alternative to the human classifier, so consistency will remain a problem.

Taxonomies

Introduction to taxonomy

The word 'taxonomy' has been with us for a very long time and it has most commonly been used in the context of classifying organisms, as in the animal kingdom classification outlined in Chapter 1. The term has more recently been borrowed by computer science and knowledge management to describe the organisation of web-based information and documentation. In this section, we move out of the traditional information and library environment by examining classification in the context of intranet and extranet development and the structuring of an organisation's digital information resources. This means that we are not focusing solely on externally published resources, but also upon an organisation's internally published documentation. However, as will be apparent, many of the issues raised are of relevance to libraries wishing to improve access to e-book and e-journal collections.

Taxonomy provides a means for building subject trees, showing the relationships between subjects in a hierarchy that can be browsed: the user can follow links down the hierarchy to more specific subjects, or follow links up the hierarchy to broader subjects. This is exactly the sort of structure traditional enumerative classification schemes like DDC impose on information, and which web directories like Yahoo and the Open Directory impose on web resources. So what taxonomy does is what library classification schemes and web directories do: it brings related subjects together and keeps them apart from unrelated subjects. The structure, as in enumerative classification schemes like Dewey Decimal, is hierarchical.

There has been an enormous interest in taxonomy in recent years with literature proliferating, particularly around the concept of the corporate taxonomy. In essence 'taxonomy' is classification which has perhaps been regarded as a rather boring topic within traditional librarianship – hence, it may be claimed, the change of name for computer scientists and knowledge managers. So if taxonomy is simply about classification, why is the concept generating so much interest? The argument is that:

> Taxonomies provide a means for designing vastly enhanced searching, browsing and filtering systems. They can be used to relieve the user from the burden of sifting specific information from the large and low-quality response of most popular search engines. Querying with respect to a taxonomy is more reliable than depending on presence or absence of specific keywords. (Chakrabarti et al., 1998)

As explained in the previous section about subject trees and web directories, taxonomies exploit the value of structured browsing as a means of information retrieval.

Taxonomy construction, maintenance and management

User-centred design

At this point it is necessary to consider user-centred perspectives in relation to taxonomy creation specifically and systems design generally. Only a brief overview of the issues is presented here, but references to various texts dealing with this area are provided in the list of recommended readings at the end of this chapter for those wishing to explore this field in greater depth.

Information systems and services have to be designed to meet the needs of library users or users within organisations. It is not possible to design effective information systems and services, including taxonomies, unless the needs of the people who will be using them have been fully researched and analysed. There is a temptation to design an elegant information structure and then hope that its potential users will embrace it. This is actually unlikely to happen if the imposed structure does not meet their expectations or needs. It may be the case that a library or an organisation invests time and expense in developing a system or taxonomy no one uses.

Taking the user-centred approach, there are four preliminary steps in the taxonomy or information system design process:

- *Information needs analysis*: find out what information the users of the system need access to. This involves determining the problems they face, and what information they need to resolve those problems.

- *Task analysis*: find out what the users of the system do when they are attempting to satisfy their information needs. This takes us into the field of search behaviour and the development of search strategies.

- *Resource analysis*: find out what individual knowledge and practical skills, for example, the users of the system employ as they complete their tasks.

- *User modelling*: identify different categories of users based on their needs, the tasks they perform and the resources they use to complete the tasks.

Allen says that:

> The goal of system design is to allow users to complete the tasks that will meet their information needs. With this in mind, system

features that will augment the resources of users when necessary will enable them to complete the tasks. Some of these features will be required by all users, while others will be required by only a portion of the user group. (Allen, 1996)

It should be clear that any library or organisation must conduct a detailed information audit or needs analysis before embarking upon the process of taxonomy creation. This is a very expensive process in terms of time and resources, but it is essential that it is done properly. Obviously the documentation itself must be fully evaluated and analysed before it can be organised within a taxonomic framework. Equally, if not more, important is an analysis of the needs and working practices of the producers and users of that documentation. Needs analysis focuses on the environment within which an information system is located and, very importantly, within which its potential users are located.

Needs analysis

A useful first step in developing an understanding of information need is to examine Maurice Line's (1974) draft definitions of information needs, wants, demands and uses. A problem with any consideration of information need is that the term itself is very imprecise. Line attempts to rid the term of its ambiguity. There is a danger that studies of information 'needs' actually explore information 'demands'. We assume that what users ask for is what they actually need, when in fact they tend to ask for what they expect the system to provide. So what we assume is an information *need* is in fact a *demand* compromised by user expectations of the information system. Line suggests that it is helpful to think of need in terms of 'what an individual ought to have, for his work, his research, his edification, his recreation, etc.' A 'want', on the other hand, is 'what an individual would like to have, whether or not the want is actually translated into a demand.' Demand is what is often assumed to be the literal expression of the need. Demand is 'what an individual asks for ... individuals may demand information they do not need, and certainly need or want information they do not demand.' Use has an obvious meaning. It is 'what an individual actually uses.' Use is of course dependent on provision. People can only use what is available, and that might represent a compromise – they might need something that their organisation's information system cannot provide.

Line's definitions underline the complexity of determining information need. If we simply ask our users what information they need, they are likely to respond with details of the information they *want*. If we rely on user requests or use studies to identify information needs, then the validity of the data we generate has been compromised by user expectations and existing information provision.

A more sophisticated approach is required. Information needs analysis tends to perceive the individual as part of their wider social and working environment, and that their individual information needs will develop through their interactions with that environment. The assumption is that by understanding the environment within which our users are located, we can predict and characterise their information needs. For an information system to be effective and to truly meet the needs of its users, there has to be an awareness of its cultural, social and organisational context.

In conducting a needs analysis in the corporate context it is useful to first map information flow within an organisation to discover what the main channels of communication are and how information transfer takes place. The channels through which information is communicated are various and emphasis has changed in recent years. A very obvious example is the increasing use of e-mail and other digital media as opposed to paper. Also it is easy to neglect the very important role of oral communication in information transfer. It may be that information transfer within an organisation could be improved by providing social spaces and an up-to-date telephone directory, rather than by redesigning more formal information retrieval mechanisms. It also has to be remembered that the organisation itself is part of a wider environment. Information flows into and out of the organisation as well as within it. Communication channels have to connect the organisation to the outside world. In other words the organisation is an open system rather than a closed one.

Having mapped information flow and examined channels of communication and information transfer, the next stage in the process of information needs analysis is applicable in both the corporate and the general library context. It is to find answers to at least three questions:

- How does the present system operate?
- What do users require from a new system?
- Will users be able to assimilate a new system, and what amount of training will be needed?

To help us find answers to these questions there are two types of research methodology we can adopt: quantitative and qualitative. Quantitative methods tend to be quicker and easier than qualitative. Using closed questions, those requiring a choice from a series of predetermined options, in questionnaires and structured interviews generates quantitative data. However, this approach also tends not to take account of the total information environment. Rohde (1986) stated: 'The quantitative approach with its emphasis on numbers and its quest for generalisation is seen as depersonalising information provision and information use and isolating them from the settings in which they occur.' The problem is that this sort of survey, while eliciting information about individual opinion, does not properly address cultural, social and environmental factors. Quantitative methods can perhaps identify information *wants, demands and uses* but may not address information *needs*.

A study by Atwood and Dervin (1981) used a three-part questionnaire with open questions to generate qualitative data. The first part of the questionnaire dealt with problems, worries and concerns respondents had experienced over the past month. The second part dealt with how a particular concern was handled or resolved. The third part asked how the participant would deal with four hypothetical situations. This kind of technique, generating in-depth qualitative data, should elicit information about the users' information requirements and how they set about satisfying them. In asking about specific work or task-related situations, a great deal can be discovered about user needs and how they are satisfied.

Project INISS (Information Needs and Information Services in Local Authority Social Services Departments: Wilson and Streatfield, 1977) used qualitative techniques: observation and interview, and although the study was conducted in the 1970s, it was exploring issues that are of major concern in knowledge management today. Wilson et al. stated:

> ... one of our basic assumptions is that information needs must be placed in the context of the ordinary working life of the subjects under investigation. The observational phase of the work provided a detailed qualitative analysis of the nature of this work and the interviews concentrated upon three aspects only:
>
> ■ the specialist knowledge possessed by the interview subjects;
>
> ■ the extent to which this knowledge was exchanged with others; and

- the effect of organizational climate on information transfer. (Wilson et al., 1979)

Again this study emphasised the importance of in-depth analysis of the individual and the organisational environment as a precursor to information systems and services design.

In practice, most user studies will employ a combination of quantitative and qualitative methods. While qualitative methods arguably produce more relevant data, qualitative research is time-consuming and costly to conduct. Whatever method is used, it is essential to conduct research about user needs and expectations before investing time and money in developing systems for retrieval of digital resources.

Task analysis

Task analysis is concerned with the search tactics or strategies employed by users when seeking information. Kuhlthau (1993) provides a model of the information search process that considers the behavioural aspects. Her model incorporates three realms:

- the *affective* realm is concerned with feeling and emotion;
- the *cognitive* realm relates to intellectual processes and problem-solving;
- the *physical* realm relates to actions.

In the context of the affective realm, users' emotional response to an information system may have a large impact on its use. If a screen display is considered unattractive, or if users become frustrated when browsing a poorly structured or maintained taxonomy, then use of the resource will decline.

The cognitive realm includes the range of keyword search and browsing strategies the user engages in. Novice users will often interrogate a database using a single keyword or simple phrase while more expert users may construct sophisticated search statements. Most searches will incorporate a range of keyword searching and browsing tactics, all of which should be identified and accommodated by an information system.

The physical realm will include how many different actions the user has to take in searching for and retrieving information. This may involve counting how many mouse clicks are needed to retrieve wanted information when browsing a taxonomy or subject tree, for example. This may seem trivial, but users are likely to discontinue their search if they have not found the information they need after four or five clicks of the mouse. From the user perspective shallow hierarchies are preferable to deep categorisation. This may not be the ideal way to represent subjects in logical or intellectual terms, but a taxonomy should be a practical aid to information retrieval.

Analysing the individual tasks that users perform when they are using an information system highlights the complexity of the information search process. A useful exercise is to use Kuhlthau's model to reflect upon the various activities one engages in when searching for information. Most of us conduct and complete an information search without thinking about the complexity of the process in which we are engaged.

Resource analysis

When the tasks people perform as they are attempting to find information have been identified, the next step is to identify the resources they use when completing those tasks. This does not mean resources in terms of printed and electronic information sources, but personal resources. People will possess different resources in their knowledge, skills and aptitudes.

User-centred system design has to allow for different levels of knowledge and skills resources in the system users. One very simple example of how these individual differences can be acknowledged is by having a command interface for expert users and a series of menu-driven interfaces for novice users. User-centred design also has to take account of individual preferences. Some users may prefer to interrogate a system directly using keywords rather than follow links in a taxonomy. Individual preferences have to be accommodated by providing a flexible search environment and perhaps a customisable interface.

User modelling

On completion of the information needs analysis, identification of the various tasks people perform when attempting to satisfy their information needs and analysis of the resources people possess, it should be possible to embody all this information in a user model or, more commonly, a set of user models. It is very difficult to design systems that will accommodate the very wide range of individual differences encountered, so there has to be an element of compromise. In other words, an attempt is made to categorise the users, identifying similarities and creating models based on those similarities. Some user modelling can be stereotyping, which is rather primitive, while other user modelling is quite sophisticated.

The search behaviour of an individual will be, to quite a great extent, determined by the nature of their information need. So perhaps the first stage, following the needs analysis, is to create categories or models of information need before attempting to analyse tasks and resources and create user models. An individual may need highly specific information (a particular document) or very general information (about a broad topic of interest). It is likely that the same individual would use different strategies to satisfy those different needs.

Taxonomy construction

How a library or an organisation structures its taxonomy is obviously dependent upon the outcomes of the information audit and the needs analysis, but it is possible to state some general principles.

The basic rule is that categories should be both exhaustive and mutually exclusive. This means that there must be an appropriate category for each subject, and only one category for each, with no subject appearing more than once in the hierarchy or subject tree. Individual electronic documents, however, can be accessed under several different subjects. It is important to note that resources in electronic form have a significant advantage over paper documents in that they have no location in physical space. In a library a book can only be shelved in one place, and if it deals with several topics, then the librarian has to decide which one topic will determine its place on the shelves. An electronic document can be in several different 'places' simultaneously.

Care must be taken in naming the categories or subjects. Any ambiguous terms should obviously be avoided. It also helps if individuals likely to use the resource have a shared understanding of terminology. That shared understanding should not, of course, be assumed, even if the taxonomy is being created for use within an organisation. Consistency is important, it might be useful to create a thesaurus or glossary of terms to provide a form of vocabulary control – this will help when documents are being added to the system and will also help in creating the subject categories themselves. Using a previous example from web directories, some have the category computing, others use the term computers. That type of inconsistency should be avoided: a decision should be made about which word form is going to be used, and it should be used consistently. It is considered good practice to use plural word form where possible (ISO, 1996).

Creating the hierarchy is a very difficult and complex task. Various automated tools are available, but the general consensus among writers in this area is that the usefulness of these tools is limited and that there should be a human element involved in taxonomy creation. A basic and obvious rule in creating the hierarchy is that subjects should be at a level in the hierarchy that reflects their relationship with other subjects – how broad or how narrow they are. Taxonomies have been described as being a hybrid of a classification scheme and a thesaurus, and indeed creating a taxonomic hierarchy is very similar to constructing a thesaurus, building up linkages of broader, narrower and related terms.

However, there is a problem with this. As previously noted, a hierarchical structure tends to break down as more subjects are added. In traditional classification terms, expressiveness suffers, with some subjects appearing at lower levels in the hierarchy than their status merits, and others appearing at higher levels. We have seen examples of this in the engineering part of the Dewey Decimal schedules. It is actually very difficult to consistently portray a subject's status by its level within the hierarchy. This is an insoluble problem: it is an inherent property of hierarchies, but an attempt must be made to maintain consistency of subdivision as far as is practicable.

As in creating a faceted classification scheme, there are traditionally two approaches to building a hierarchy – the top-down and the bottom-up. There is often a temptation to begin by naming the top-level categories and then working down through the various levels until the most specific subject descriptors are reached. A better approach may be to start with the specific and then work up to the general. As well as the top-down and the bottom-up, a third approach has been suggested: the middle-out (Uschold and Gruninger, 1996). Here it is suggested that the process should begin with a definition of the most fundamental or basic terms before seeking more general and more specific terms. So, for example, classification would be identified as a basic term and that could lead to broader terms such as cataloguing and narrower terms such as DDC and LCC.

Maintenance of the taxonomy

A concept that has been explored in the context of traditional classification schemes is that of hospitality. A taxonomy, like any classification scheme, must be able to accommodate new subjects as they arise. Also new documents must be classified and added to the collection as in any library. Creation of the taxonomy is only the first step in providing a useful information resource, once created it must be maintained.

Creating new categories

This should not be done on an ad-hoc basis. Vocabulary control is important here to help maintain consistency of naming if new categories have to be created. But the first question ought to be, is a new category needed or can this document be accommodated within an existing category or categories? If care was taken in creating the taxonomy in the first place, then some developments could have been anticipated and categories created accordingly.

Adding categories to the hierarchy

If new categories are created than they have to be accommodated within the existing hierarchy of subjects. The problem is that the hierarchy will almost certainly start to break down as new categories are added. It may be that one part of the hierarchy is expanding enormously while other parts remain relatively stable. In this case, a decision has to be made as to whether it is appropriate to expand vertically or if expansion should be horizontal. Consistency of subdivision is important here and ensuring that a category's level within the hierarchy reflects its relationship with others. However, as previously noted, studies have shown that shallow hierarchies are preferred by users. If users of a subject tree or taxonomy have not found the wanted information after drilling down through four links then they are likely to abandon the search. Horizontal expansion, therefore, while perhaps not achieving the most accurate representation or elegant structure, would be more likely to meet the needs and expectations of users.

Adding documents

Here we are moving beneath the surface level and looking at the electronic resources themselves.

Precise classification of documents is perhaps not as crucial in the electronic environment as it is in the traditional library environment. A single document can be linked to and retrieved via several different categories to allow for individual needs and expertise. However, it is not good practice to overload the system with links because that will affect its use. Effort must be made to ensure that inappropriate or redundant links are not included. It will take users longer to find what they need if they are bombarded with irrelevant information when they explore a category.

Removing documents

So far the focus has been upon adding resources to a taxonomy, but it has already been suggested that a taxonomy loses its efficiency as more categories and resources are added to it. Is it therefore necessary to remove redundant categories and dated documents or those which are no longer relevant? The answer is obvious. Maintaining a taxonomy is like maintaining any library – materials have to be removed or weeded as well as added. Information in electronic form, perhaps to a greater degree than information in traditionally published documents, is often of transient value and out-of-date materials must be removed. All links to a category or document must also be deleted when it is removed otherwise dead links become a problem and will frustrate users.

Taxonomy management

The issue of managing a taxonomy generates a series of questions and possible answers. Here discussion is centred around the management of a corporate taxonomy, with the emphasis on internally generated documentation. However, many of the issues would apply in the general library context.

Who should be responsible for maintenance? Ideally a librarian or information manager should have overarching responsibility for managing the taxonomy. If everyone within an organisation can add what they like where they like, then a nicely structured search and retrieval tool descends into chaos.

Who should be responsible for deciding what is included? Again, it seems sensible that a librarian or information manager, as someone with an overview of the whole organisation and its needs and the needs of individual members of staff, should be responsible for deciding what resources are included, and of course, how the resources are indexed – which categories resources should be allocated to. It would be preferable to give the originators of documents responsibility for indexing, but individual authors may not be consistent in how they name and categorise materials. A list of subject descriptors or a thesaurus could help to increase consistency but it would be safer to place responsibility for indexing in the hands of an information specialist or team. The approach taken would ultimately depend upon the volume of work.

This leads on to another question: should everything be included? If the answer is yes, then that dispenses with the need for someone to make decisions about what is included. But organisations can generate enormous amounts of documentation – is it sensible to have everything accessible to everyone? Taxonomies are a means of improving resource sharing and information retrieval. If they grow too large or too complex or if they contain a lot of documentation which is of no possible interest to the majority of users, then they lose their efficiency as information retrieval tools.

This leads to another question: who has access? Does everyone have access to everything? Is there a need for a single taxonomy for the whole organisation or is it more appropriate to have a shared taxonomy plus a series of specialist taxonomies? This may seem to be contrary to the idea of a taxonomy as a tool to facilitate resource sharing, but it may be that some parts of the organisation are sufficiently specialised to merit their own smaller, highly specialised taxonomies to facilitate resource sharing among a few highly specialised individuals. Some resources may only be for the eyes of certain people within the organisation, in which case parts of the taxonomy will have to be closed to groups of users. It has also been assumed thus far in this section that the taxonomy will be mounted on an organisation's intranet, but it may be appropriate to mount parts of it on an extranet. This introduces a set of new issues around public access and security.

Who should be responsible for deciding what should be removed? Should the taxonomy manager decide, or should the creators of documents decide? If a librarian or taxonomy manager is responsible for deciding what is added then it seems logical that they should be responsible for what is removed. This decision may be straightforward if, for example, an interim report is being superseded by a final report, but a taxonomy manager may lack sufficient specialist knowledge to decide when a document contains out-of-date and possibly misleading information. Perhaps specialist staff should be involved in the weeding process, sending suggestions about what should be deleted to the taxonomy manager.

To conclude, one thing which should be apparent is that building and maintaining a taxonomy is a very complex task, and a great deal of thought has to go into the process. In the general enthusiasm about getting involved with taxonomy creation, organisations have not necessarily grasped the complexity of what they are taking on. Organisations have built taxonomies on the basis of what they think they need, without undertaking a thorough analysis of needs, or they have built taxonomies based on what a commercial package can provide. In the general enthusiasm, two basic questions are sometimes neglected: what benefit will this provide and do we need this?

Ontologies

This concept has recently been generating much interest and literature. However, it is an unfamiliar and perhaps confusing concept to many and it is helpful to explain and, to some extent, demystify it in the context of classification of digital resources. A dictionary definition of ontology is 'the branch of metaphysics that deals with the nature and essence of things or of existence' (*Chambers Dictionary*, 1999). This is not particularly useful and helps to confuse rather than to clarify. Gruber's commonly cited definition (1993) of an ontology as 'a specification of a conceptualisation' places it within the discipline of knowledge and information management rather than philosophy but does little to explain its meaning.

A more detailed definition places ontology firmly within the context of classification and thesaurus construction: 'An ontology is a document or file that formally defines the relations among terms. The most typical kind of ontology for the Web has a taxonomy and a set of inference rules' (Berners-Lee et al., 2001). As we have already explored, a taxonomy consists of the hierarchical display of a series of classes and subclasses. The inference rules in an ontology add value and sophistication to a taxonomy.

An example of an inference rule using the animal kingdom taxonomy from Chapter 1 would be:

> If X belongs in the subphylum Y, and Z is an X, then Z also belongs in the subphylum Y. A specific instance would be: if a mammal belongs in the subphylum Vertebrata, and a dog is a mammal, then a dog also belongs in the subphylum Vertebrata.

An example using 614.57 in the DDC schedules would be:

> If 614.57 is the notation for bacterial diseases, and Lyme disease
> has the notation 614.5746, then Lyme disease must be a bacterial
> disease.

The inclusion of inference rules would allow a system to support hierarchically expanded searching: if the user is interested in this concept, then they would probably be interested in these related concepts.

The power of the ontology can be increased with the inclusion of equivalence relationships. An example might be: TV is equivalent to television. When a user is searching for information the equivalence relationship would map the user's query onto other terms representing the same concept, dispensing with the need for the user to specify synonymous terms in a search statement.

Inference rules serve the same purpose as a hierarchically structured classification scheme or thesaurus, making explicit how concepts are logically related to each other. Equivalence relationships serve the same purpose as *see* or *use* references in an index or thesaurus to control vocabulary and eliminate synonyms. The concept of an ontology may seem unfamiliar to librarians, but in fact it is intimately related to classification and thesaurus construction.

Soergel made this very clear when he wrote of ontologies:

> A classification by any other name is still a classification. The use
> of a different term is symptomatic of the lack of communication
> between scientific communities. The vast body of knowledge on
> classification structure and on ways to display classifications ...
> and the huge intellectual capital embodied in many classification
> schemes' thesauri is largely ignored. (Soergel, 1999)

He then went on to provide examples of ontologies[1] that would have benefited from the application of principles of classification and thesaurus construction.

It is not relevant here to enter into an in-depth discussion of ontologies, but it was considered necessary to demystify the term as we are likely to increasingly encounter it in the knowledge and information management literature. Those willing to explore the concept further can find literature on this topic cited in the references and in the recommended readings at the end of this chapter. Unfortunately, it seems that librarianship and information science have, as was also the case with taxonomies, been ignored by the computing and artificial intelligence communities when devising more powerful search tools, resulting in unnecessary duplication of work in devising principles that were already long-established. This level of invisibility is not to our credit as a profession.

Overview

In this chapter we have explored classification of digital resources with an explanation of subject trees, taxonomies and ontologies. We have seen that these topics are very closely related to traditional library classification even though they are often covered in different disciplines like computer science and knowledge management.

Subject trees, taxonomies and ontologies possess characteristics of both hierarchical or expressive classification and thesauri. They provide a structured browsing environment, make explicit conceptual relationships between subject areas and promote vocabulary control. To make these linkages clear, thesaurus construction and browsing strategies were examined in some detail.

Something that should be clear is that the needs of the users are paramount when designing information structures for the electronic environment. It is not sufficient to create elegant information structures; we have to take a pragmatic approach, even if the result offends the classification theorist. Analysis of user needs and acknowledgement of individual differences were explored in the section on taxonomy as were the practical implications of taxonomy creation, maintenance and management.

Note

1. Ontologies: links to many examples can be found at: *www.daml.org/ontologies/submitter.html*. An ontology specifically cited by Soergel (1999) is: WordNet: *www.cogsci.princeton.edu/~wn*.

References

Allen, B.L. (1996) *Information Tasks: Toward a User-Centered Approach to Information Systems*. London: Academic Press, pp. 49–50.

Attwood, R. and Dervin, B. (1982) 'Challenges to sociocultural predictors of information seeking', in *Communication Yearbook 5,* ed. M. Burgoon. Piscataway, NJ: Transaction, pp. 549–69.

Berners-Lee, T. et al. (2001) 'The semantic web', *Scientific American,* 17 May.

Chakrabarti, S. et al. (1998) 'Scalable feature selection, classification and signature generation for organizing large text databases into hierarchical topic taxonomies', *VLDB Journal,* 7, 163–78.

Chambers 21st Century Dictionary (1999) Edinburgh: Chambers.

Gruber, T.R. (1993) 'A translation approach to portable ontologies', *Knowledge Acquisition,* 5(2), 199–220.

International Organization for Standardization (1996) ISO 999:1996: *Information and documentation: guidelines for the content, organization and presentation of indexes.* Geneva: ISO.

Kuhlthau, C.C. (1993) *Seeking Meaning.* Westport, CT: Ablex.

Line, M.B. (1974) 'Draft definitions: information and library needs, wants, demands and uses', *Aslib Proceedings,* 26(2), 87.

Meadow, C.T. (1970) *Man–Machine Communication.* London: Wiley, p. 124.

Rohde, N.F. (1986) 'Information needs', in *Advances in Librarianship,* Vol. 14. London: Academic Press, pp. 49–73.

Rowley, J. (1992) *Organizing Knowledge: An Introduction to Information Retrieval,* 2nd edn. Aldershot: Gower, p. 252.

Soergel, D. (1999) 'The rise of ontologies or the reinvention of classification', *Journal of the American Society for Information Science,* 50(12), 1119–20.

Uschold, M. and Gruninger, M. (1996) 'Ontologies: principles, methods and applications', *Knowledge Engineering Review,* 11(2), 93–155.

Wilson, T.D. and Streatfield, D.R. (1977) 'Information needs in local authority social services departments: an interim report on Project INISS', *Journal of Documentation,* 33(4), 277–93.

Wilson, T.D. et al. (1979) 'Information needs in local authority social services departments: a second report on Project INISS', *Journal of Documentation,* 35(2), 120–36.

Recommended reading

The above books and articles provide excellent coverage of particular aspects of this area and are also recommended. Good, basic texts that together provide good coverage of all the issues discussed in this chapter are:

Aitchison, J. et al. (1997) *Thesaurus Construction and Use: A Practical Manual*, 3rd edn. London: Aslib.

Allen, B.L. (1996) *Information Tasks: Toward a User-Centered Approach to Information Systems*. London: Academic Press.

Gilchrist, A. (2004) *Information Architecture: Designing Information Environments for Purpose*. London: Facet.

Marcella, R. and Maltby, A. (2000) *The Future of Classification*. Aldershot: Gower.

Rosenfeld, L. and Morville, P. (2002) *Information Architecture for the World Wide Web*, 2nd edn. Sebastopol, CA: O'Reilly.

Shneiderman, B. (1998) *Designing the User Interface: Strategies for Effective Human Computer Interaction*, 3rd edn. Harlow: Addison-Wesley.

Summary

Classification theory and library classification schemes

Classification as a subject within library science is often perceived as being difficult and requiring highly developed technical and analytical skills. While this is true up to a point, the ability to classify is something that we all possess, and we interact with formal classification schemes on a daily basis. We would be unable to function effectively if we did not classify our world. Bowker and Star (2000) explain that:

> To classify is human ... we all spend large parts of our days doing classification work, often tacitly, and we make up and use a range of ad hoc classifications to do so. We sort dirty dishes from clean, white laundry from colorfast, important e-mail to be answered from e-junk.

This places classification firmly within the realm of the mundane – it is something that provides natural order in our everyday lives. When we go to the supermarket, we are largely unaware that we are interacting with a sophisticated formal classification scheme. Products on supermarket shelves have been organised using the same principles as books on library shelves, yet the supermarket classification (usually) seems natural and comfortable to navigate, while the library classification seems complicated and difficult to grasp. In the supermarket apples and oranges are shelved separately but near each other, with furniture polish shelved in a different part of the store. In the library books on property law and criminal law are shelved separately but near each other, with books on medicine shelved in a different part of the library. Both classifications recognise similarities and differences and organise stock accordingly.

The key to easy navigation in the supermarket and in the library is familiarity.

In library classification schemes subjects are represented by a code: the notation. The notation is used to establish shelf order and is a very effective means of expressing the content of books accurately and succinctly. The notation introduces a level of abstraction that needs to be fully understood only by expert classifiers, not by the library users. However, we all deal with abstractions in our everyday lives: we learn telephone numbers, post codes, PIN numbers, the numbers of bus routes, the numbers of television channels, and so on. Again, when the abstraction becomes familiar perceived complexity is reduced.

Classification schemes for general collections

Dewey Decimal Classification and Library of Congress Classification are the two most widely used classification schemes and both are very effective tools for organising materials in public and academic libraries. Neither scheme is perfect, but advantages outweigh disadvantages. Both schemes have been used successfully for many years and benefit from good levels of support and regular revisions.

	Advantages	Disadvantages
DDC	■ Familiarity ■ Up-to-date coverage	■ Uneven coverage in some disciplines ■ Rigid structure and lack of flexibility
LCC	■ Detailed listing of subjects ■ Excellent hospitality	■ Notations can be long and complicated ■ Subject listing is dependent on the holdings of the Library of Congress

Classification schemes for specialist collections

Universal Decimal Classification provides admirable depth of description for specialised subjects because of the very flexible way in which notational elements can be combined. However, a general scheme may not provide the most efficient means of classifying materials in libraries with narrow subject coverage. Special classification schemes based on faceted principles can be created to meet the needs of a particular collection. Such schemes can be easy to compile and may provide a practical alternative to existing published classifications.

	Advantages	Disadvantages
UDC	■ Depth of classification ■ Mnemonic qualities ■ Flexibility	■ Complexity of citation and filing order ■ Long notations
Special schemes	■ Tailored to meet local needs ■ Can be created to possess desirable qualities like simplicity of notation	■ Unfamiliar to new users ■ Reclassification and recataloguing of materials

Classifying electronic resources

Librarians have a long history of organising and providing access to information and are trained to work with searching, browsing, and indexing technologies. Forward-looking librarians (sometimes described as 'cybrarians') see that their expertise applies in new arenas far beyond the library walls. (Rosenfeld and Morville, 2002)

Digital information resources benefit from classification in the same way as traditional library resources. Subject trees, taxonomies and ontologies in the digital information environment bear many similarities to library classification schemes and thesauri. Information architecture incorporates elements of traditional library technical services, with classification seen as core in improving the effectiveness of retrieval systems. Subject trees and taxonomies utilise hierarchies to encourage structured browsing of digital resources in much the same way as classification schemes like DDC facilitate browsing of materials on library shelves. Ontologies can provide an additional layer of semantic association by establishing inference and equivalence relationships in much the same way as a thesaurus.

Endnote

Hopefully this book has increased the readers' familiarity with library classification schemes and the technical terminology associated with them. Some technical aspects of the subject were not examined, as the main purpose of the book was to demystify a complex topic within librarianship and to encourage the development of practical skills in using the major library classification schemes. Additionally in Chapter 4 we have seen how classification is being applied in the digital environment. Far from being solely a concern of the librarian, classification is a dynamic and exciting subject that impacts on many aspects of our lives, from writing a report to downloading tracks to an iPod.

Classification has been a rather neglected discipline in recent years. It is sometimes seen as a necessary evil to be studied (not necessarily in-depth) at Library School and then avoided as far as possible in professional life. Perhaps computer science and knowledge management will be responsible for reviving interest in the subject. Now that classifiers can legitimately call themselves information architects, classification will come to be regarded as a challenging and exciting professional skill.

References

Bowker, G.C. and Star, S.L. (2000) *Sorting Things Out: Classification and Its Consequences*. Cambridge, MA: MIT Press, pp. 1–2.

Rosenfeld, L. and Morville, P. (2002) *Information Architecture for the World Wide Web*, 2nd edn. Sebastopol, CA: O'Reilly, p. 19.

Appendix
Answers to practical exercises

Throughout, explanations are provided where appropriate.

Dewey Decimal Classification (22nd edn)

The DDC notations represent:

070.5797   Electronic publications (digital publications)

973.3115   Boston Tea Party

133.3337   Feng shui

248.8431   Guide to Christian life for mothers

The Christianity schedules provide very detailed coverage. The same detail is not present in the coverage of any other religion

681.145   Manufacture of calculators

Calculators have been taken out of standing room and assigned their own notation

621.388337   Maintenance and repair of video recorders and recordings

One would probably assume that this is a built number because of its length. That is not the case – it simply comes from a very crowded part of the schedules

551.461364   Geomorphology of the Gulf of Mexico

Number building has already been applied here. To the base number 551.461 has been added the last three digits of the notation for the Gulf of Mexico from Table 2: 16364

338.4766342	The brewing industry
338.47	Services and specific products (economics)
66342	Beer and ale (from 663.42)

Instructions at 338.47001–.47999 tell us that we can add any number from the DDC schedules to specify a service or product

| 822.3 | English drama of the Elizabethan period |

Another example of a built number in the schedules

372.72044	Teaching of arithmetic in elementary education
372	Elementary education
.72	Arithmetic
044	Teaching (from a table of special topics at 372.3–372.8)

614.534	Incidence of leishmaniasis
614.53	Incidence of protozoan infections
4	Leishmaniasis (the number following 616.936 in 616.9362–616.9364)

398.24529773	Folk literature about wolves
398.2452	Folk literature about real animals
9773	Wolves (numbers following 59 in 592–599)

025.52774	Reference and information services in public libraries
025.527	Reference and information services in specific types of institutions
74	Public libraries (the numbers following 02 in 026–027)

305.4302092	Women librarians
305.43	Women's occupations
0209	Library and information sciences, historical, geographic, persons treatment
2	Persons (from –092 in Table 1)

427.88	Dialects of Northumberland
427	English language, geographic variations
88	Northumberland (numbers following 42 in 421–428 from Table 2)

639.3757	Trout farming
639.37	Culture of specific kinds of fishes
57	Trout (the numbers following 597 in 597.2–597.7)

599.361565	Hibernation of squirrels
599.36	Squirrels
1	Base number for general topics of natural history of animals from 592–599
565	The numbers following 591 representing hibernation

785.7194	String quartet
785.7	String ensembles
19	Size of ensemble (from table at 785.2–785.9)
4	Quartet (from 785.14)

Effective use is made of literal mnemonics here

DDC notations:

Human physiology	612
Animal behaviour	591.5
Visual perception	152.14
Encyclopaedia of medicine	610.3

Add to base number for medicine, 61, notation 03 from Table 1 to indicate an encyclopaedia

| Neurophysiology | 612.8 |
| Book of Common Prayer | 264.03 |

Classed under public worship, Anglican churches

German grammar   435

> *An example of a built number in the schedules. The notation for Grammar from Table 4 has been added to the base number for the German language: 43*

How to play bridge   795.415

> *The notation for comprehensive works on the card game*

Education of gifted children   371.95

Winter cookery   641.564

> *Notation for seasonal cooking*

Research methods in organic chemistry   547.0072

> *Standard subdivisions are preceded by two zeros in this part of the schedules*

The Koran (English translation)   297.122521

> *The notation for the English language from Table 6: 21, has been added to the base number for translations of the Koran: 297.1225*

Word for Windows manual   005.52

History of the trade union movement   331.8809

> *Notation from Table 1 indicating historical treatment has been added to base number 331.88*

Ethics of human cloning   176

> *Classed under ethics of sex and reproduction*

The Prelude by William Wordsworth   821.7

> *Add to base number 821, English poetry, the number 7 to specify the Romantic period. From the period table at 820.1–828*

Information retrieval systems in pharmacology   025.066151

> *Add to base number 025.06: Information storage and retrieval systems devoted to specific disciplines and subjects, the notation for pharmacology: 6151*

Richard Feynman: a biography   530.92 or 539.092

Add to the base number for physics: 53, notation 092 from Table 1 to specify persons treatment. As Feynman was particularly associated with quantum physics an alternative location would be at 539.092: modern physics, persons treatment. An option would be to class all biographies in the 920s, in which case the notation would be: 925.3 or 925.39

Drug treatment of Parkinson's disease   616.833061

Add to base number for Parkinson's disease: 616.833, notation 061 from a table of special auxiliaries at 616.1–616.9

Howard Hodgkin: paintings   759.2

Notation for an English painter

Nurse education in the United States   610.73071073

Add to base number for nursing: 610.73, notation 071 from Table 1, then follow the instructions to indicate a geographic treatment by adding 0, then notation 73 from Table 2 to specify United States

Statistical methods in psychology   150.727

Add to base number for psychology: 15, notation 0727 from Table 1

Fashion in Restoration England   391.0094209032

Add to the base number for costume: 391, notation 009 to specify historical and geographic treatment. Go to Table 1 at –093–099 to find instructions on how to add notations for England and Restoration period. Add 42 from Table 2 to specify England. Add 09 for historical treatment. Go to Table 1 at 0901–0905 to find notation for the Restoration period. Add 032 to specify 17th century.

An optional notation constructed using instructions at –093–099 in Table 1 would be: 391.009420066

Add to 391.00942 (as constructed above), 0, then add the number following 941 in the history schedules to specify the Restoration period: 066

Films of Orson Welles   791.430233092

The built number for motion picture directors is actually included in the relative index. It is constructed as follows. Add to base number 791.43: motion pictures, notation from Table 1 as modified under 792.01–792.02. Direction is at 792.0233, so we add 0233 to the base number and then add 092 from Table 1 to indicate a person's treatment

Library of Congress Classification

LCC classifications

There is no attempt to explain each notation in detail here, as notation building has not been necessary.

Human physiology   QP34.5

    QP: Physiology

Animal behaviour   QL751

    QL: Zoology

Visual perception   QP475

    QP: Physiology

Encyclopaedia of medicine   RC81

    RC: Internal medicine

Neurophysiology   QP355

    QP: Physiology

Book of Common Prayer   BX5943

    BX: Christian denominations

German grammar   PF3112

    PF: West Germanic languages

How to play bridge   GV1282.3

    GV: Recreation, leisure

Education of gifted children   LC3997

    LC: Special aspects of education

Winter cookery   TX714

    TX: Home economics

Research methods in organic chemistry   QD256

    QD: Chemistry

The Koran (English translation)   BP109

    BP: Islam, Bahaism, theosophy, etc.

Word for Windows manual   QA76.76 or Z52.5

    QA: Mathematics

    Z: Books (general), writing, paleography

    Two notations are possible here. Works on word processing packages could be classed under computer sciences in Mathematics, or under word processing in class Z

History of the trade union movement   HD6475

    HD: Industries, land use, labour

Ethics of human cloning   QH442.2

    QH: Natural history, biology

The Prelude by William Wordsworth   PR5864

    PR: English literature

Information retrieval   ZA3075

    ZA: Information resources

Richard Feynman: a biography   QC16.F49

    QC: Physics

Drug treatment of Parkinson's disease   QP905 or RC382

    QP: Physiology

    RC: Internal medicine

Pharmacology is classed within physiology. Parkinson's disease is classed within internal medicine, diseases of the nervous system. Either notation would be acceptable, depending on the focus of the work

Howard Hodgkin: paintings   ND497.H63

    ND: Painting

Nurse education   RT81

    RT: Nursing

Statistical methods in psychology   BF39

    BF: Psychology

Fashion in Restoration England   GT735

    GT: Manners and customs

Films of Orson Welles   PN1998.3.W45

    PN: Literature (general)

Works on motion pictures generally and on specific directors are classed in the Literature schedules

Universal Decimal Classification (pocket edition)

The UDC notations represent:

621.39	Telecommunications engineering
639.3	Fish breeding/farming
785.7	Chamber music
025.5:027.4	Information services in public libraries
004.08:655.4	Optical media, publishing
53/54(035)	Handbook of physics and chemistry
94(73)"1773"	History of the United States, 1773
305–055.2	Women's studies

241–055.52–055.2	Moral theology for mothers
551.4(261.6)	Geomorphology of the South Atlantic ocean and connected seas
821.111–2"15/16"	Drama in the English language in the 16th and 17th centuries
372.8:511	Elementary school education, arithmetic
578.7:614.4	Viral diseases, prevention and control
398.2:599.742.1	Folk tales about canines (dogs, wolves, etc.)
811.11'282	Dialects of the English language
599.322:591.5	Squirrels, behaviour
(038)=134.2	Spanish dictionary
395(=521)	Japanese people, etiquette and manners

UDC notations:

Human physiology	612
Visual perception	159.931
Encyclopaedia of medicine	61(031)

61 is the base number for medical sciences. (031) is the notation for encyclopaedias from Table 1d: Common auxiliaries of form

Book of Common Prayer	264:283.1

Liturgy in relation to Anglican churches, the colon linking the two notations to indicate a relationship

German grammar	811.112.2'36

The base notation for Languages is 811. To this is added the notation for German, derived from Table 1c, replacing the equals sign with a point: .112.2. The notation for grammar, '36, is taken from a list of special auxiliaries at 81, linguistics and languages

How to play bridge	794.41
Education of gifted children	37–056.31IQ130

The base number for education is 37. To this is added a notation from Table 1k: Common auxiliaries of persons and personal characteristics: –056.31, persons according to intelligence. To this can be added a non-UDC notation indicating Intelligence Quotient. A commonly agreed definition of 'gifted' is an IQ of 130 and above

Winter cookery   641.5"324"

The base number for cookery is 641.5. To this can be added a notation from Table 1g: Common auxiliaries of time: "324" is the notation for winter

History of the Soviet Union 1953 to 1991   94(47+57)"1953/1991"

The base number for history is 94. To this can be added the notation for place from Table 1e: (47+57) and the time notation: "1953/1991"

Research methods in organic chemistry   547(076) or
                                           547:001.89

The base number for organic chemistry is 547. To this can be added either notation (076) from Table 1d: Common auxiliaries of form, or notation 001.89 from the main schedules: Organisation of scientific work and research

The Koran (English translation)   297:291.8=111

The base number for Islam is 297. To this is added notation for sacred books: 291.8. To specify English language version, add notation =111 from Table 1c: Common auxiliaries of language

Word for Windows manual   004.91(035)WORD

The base number for word processing is 004.91. To this is added the Table 1d notation for manual: (035), and the name of the word processing package

History of the trade union movement   331.105.44(091)

The base number for trade unions is 331.105.44 (an example of the point being used to break up a number every third digit). To this is added the notation for historical treatment, (091), from Table 1d: Common auxiliaries of form

Ethics of human cloning   176 or 174:57

The first notation, for sexual ethics, places this subject at the same location as DDC. An alternative may be to class this work under occupational ethics, 174, and add the notation for the biological sciences, 57

The Prelude by William Wordsworth   821.111–1
                                                       WORDSWORTH

The base notation for literature is 821. To this is added .111 to specify the English language. Next is added a special auxiliary, from a list at 82, to denote poetry: –1. Finally, the author's name is added. It is acceptable to use an abbreviated version of the name, e.g. WORD. In a library with an extensive collection of literature, it would be desirable to specify nationality to differentiate between English literature in the English language and American literature in the English language for example. In this case an area notation from Table 1e would be inserted: 821.111–1(410.1)WORDSWORTH

Richard Feynman: a biography   53(092)
                                                       530.145(092)
                                                       929:53 or
                                                       929:53.145

There are several alternatives here. Depending on library policy, biographies can be shelved with their subject or shelved together. The subject is either physics, 53, or quantum theory, 530.145, to which is added (092), to specify biography, from Table 1d. The notation for biography in the main schedules is 929, to which is added the notation for physics or quantum theory

Howard Hodgkin: paintings   75HODGKIN

The base number for painting is 75, to which is added the artist's name. As in the Wordsworth example, it is possible to arrange by country: 75(410.1)HODGKIN

Nurse education in the United States   377:616–051(73)

The base number for vocational and technical education is 377. To this is added the notation for nurses (medicine: 616, persons as agents: –051 from Table 1k) and the notation for the United States (73) from Table 1e

Fashion in Restoration England   391(410.1)"1660/1685"

> *The base number for fashion is 391. To this is added the notation for England from Table 1e: (410.1). Finally a period notation is added, with "1660/1685" signifying the Restoration period, the reign of Charles II*

Films of Orson Welles   791.43.071WELLES

> *The base number for films is 791.43. To this is added a special auxiliary for directors, from the .0 auxiliaries at 7. Finally the name is added*

Classification scheme for a photographic library

Brixton riots, 1981	Hc Ln Brixton 1981
University graduation ceremony, 2004	Ab Hb 2004
Regent Street Christmas lights, 1987	Hs Ld Regent St 1987
Football players, Hackney Marshes, 1930s	Da Ll 193
Houses of Parliament	Ad La
Funfair at Battersea Park, 1950s	Df Le Battersea 195
Petticoat Lane market, 2001	Bl Ld Petticoat Lane 2001
Anti-war rally, Hyde Park, 2003	Hd Le 2003
Street entertainers, Covent Garden, 1994	Dj Ld Covent Garden 1994
Big Issue seller, Strand, 2002	Kx Ld Strand 2002

Specific place names can be included as required to create an alphabetical arrangement.

Index